Reproduced from 'Treningsboka' by kind permission of the author

ORIENTEERING

ORIENTEERING

by
JOHN DISLEY

ILLUSTRATED BY
GORDON MANSELL

FABER AND FABER
London

First published in 1967
by Faber and Faber Limited
24 Russell Square London W.C.1
Reprinted April 1967
Reprinted 1968
Revised edition 1969
Printed in Great Britain by
Latimer Trend & Co Ltd Whitstable

SBN 571 08987 9 (paper edition)
SBN 571 08031 6 (cloth edition)

To
GEOFFREY DYSON

*who, by his inspired coaching, convinced me
that a game is all the better for being
played properly; and who, seventeen years ago,
came back from a visit to Sweden with a story
about a sport that was threatening the life-
blood of Swedish middle-distance running. He
said it was called orienteering, and gave me
a Silva compass.
The seed planted in 1949 took a long time to
germinate. I hope, Geoff, that this flower
is to your liking.*

Acknowledgements and Thanks

To the Officers and Committee of the British Orienteering Federation for their tremendous co-operation and assistance in the compilation of the Rules of Competition, Control Terminology and the Constitution. This work was all original and much midnight oil was burnt during its conception, especially by my good friends Christopher Brasher, the Chairman, and Gerald Charnley, the Secretary, of the B.O.F.

To the 'Silva' company, through Jan Kjellström—a fine young ambassador for the sport, who came, saw and won two of our major competitions in 1965, for much help and information on the history and modern state of the sport in Scandinavia.

To Mr. B. J. Ward, who through the past five years has worked persistently to see the sport of orienteering established in England. His help to schools during this period has also been outstanding.

To the following publications for ideas and information: *The Sport of Orienteering*, *Know the Game—Orienteering*, *Treningsboka*, *Nya Bänlaggar-boken* and the 'Silva' instructional pamphlets.

To the Controller of H.M. Stationery Office for his sanction to reproduce from the Ordnance Survey Maps, Crown Copyright Reserved.

'. . . orienteering is not a treasure hunt.'

Contents

1. THE SPORT OF ORIENTEERING   *page* 15
   Explanation and justification. History and origins
   in Sweden—in Europe—in Britain. Position today.

2. GETTING STARTED   26
   Description of a novice cross-country event. Typical
   Fixture List. The map notes. Control card and
   sheet. Procedure during a race—after the race.

3. THE MAP   39
   Types of map. The 1 : 25000 scale map. The new
   second series map. Marginal information on orien-
   teering map sheet. Four and six figure references.
   Romer construction and use. The map symbols.
   Contour lines. Magnetic variation. Code of ethics.
   Copyright.

4. THE COMPASS   51
   The function of the compass. The Silva compass.
   Bearings. Compass work part I—which direction?
   Taking grid bearings. Converting bearings. Travel
   on a bearing. Compass work part II—where am I?
   Taking a magnetic bearing. Finding position by
   bearings. Setting the map—by reference to the
   terrain—by using a compass. Back bearings. Four
   right angles technique.

5. DECISION MAKING   67
   Choice of routes—long, easy way *v.* short, tough
   route. Height climbed *v.* detour round. Use of
   guide lines. Collecting features. Aiming-off. Determining distances. Step counting.

6. TYPES OF ORIENTEERING COMPETITION   78
   Score events—general organization, team competition. Cross-country orienteering. Control terminology—definition of features. Night orienteering
   —safety. Relay racing. Line orienteering. Code of
   conduct.

CONTENTS

7. PRACTICAL TRAINING GAMES   93
Miniature score event. Point orienteering. Compass practices—hunt the silver dollar. Miniature orienteering.

8. ORIENTEERING EQUIPMENT   98
Clothing and footwear. Compasses. Tachometer. Watch. Headlamp. Control markers. Marking stamps. Maps—copying machines, reproductions, royalties.

9. SETTING THE COURSE   109
Fundamental principles. Suitable terrain. Correcting the map. Selecting the problems. The control site. Positioning the marker flag.

10. THE ORGANIZATION OF A COMPETITION   122
The competition rules. Check list for championship event—for inter-club event. Control cards. Recorder's sheet. Control description sheet. Instructions to competitors. Control sheet for a score event. The start area. The control sites. The finish.

11. FITNESS TRAINING FOR ORIENTEERING   146
Basic running training. Interval running. Continuous running. Fartlek. Terrain negotiation. The training diary.

12. THE LAST WORD   155

APPENDIX I: British Orienteering Federation Constitution   156

APPENDIX II: The Names and Addresses of Association Secretaries   161

APPENDIX III: Bibliography   163

APPENDIX IV: Copying Services   165

APPENDIX V: Duke of Edinburgh's Award Scheme   166

INDEX   169

Illustrations

(*between pages 80 and 81*)

1. The Author
2. The basic equipment needed by the orienteer
3. Master-maps set up on trestles
4. The parts of the 'Silva' compass
5. Lieut. Griffiths at the master-maps
6. Two boys work out their salvation
7. A girl competitor sets her map at a control point
8. At the control in a night event.
9. A section of a Swiss map
10. A section of a Swedish map
11. A section of a French map
12. Senior men competitors copy down information
13. Chris Brasher moves away from a control point
14. Two competitors at a 'food-station'
15. The recorder checks a control card

The author acknowledges his thanks for permission to reproduce the following illustrations: Nos. 1 and 2 by courtesy of the *Daily Mail*; Nos. 3, 5, 12, 14, Jan Kjellström; No. 4, 'Silva' company; No. 6, R. Austin; No. 7, Mayerhaff; No. 13, *Times Educational Supplement*; Nos. 8, 9, 10, 11, 15, Copyright the Author.
Aerial photograph, Crown Copyright Reserved.

List of Maps

(*between pages 48 and 49*)

1. A Master copy for an Event

2 and 3. Control Terminology and Definition of Features

4. Map Symbols for the $2\frac{1}{2}''$ to the mile scale map

5. A section of a modern Swedish map

6. The Master-map for a Line Orienteering Event

7. The Master-map for the Novices' Event

8, 9 and 10. Map Symbols for the new Second Series Ordnance Survey maps

11. Control sites for a Score Event

12. Comparison of map and aerial photograph of terrain

1

The Sport of Orienteering

In this sophisticated age plain physical exercise is seldom enough to satisfy on its own; 'keeping the weight down' is hardly a continued excuse week after week for a brisk Sunday afternoon trot or a wandering plod over the local common. Consequently, even though we preach the value of fitness, many of us soon ask the civilized question, 'Fitness for what?', and tend to direct our exertions to just satisfying our modest daily and weekly physical needs.

Most of us, and this includes even our most renowned track and field stars, are more inclined to enjoy physical exertion if it is pushed into the semi-conscious part of the mind by mental exercise. This can be done by the strain of personal competition or by the technicality of the event. A long-distance runner of the 1920's who was also a mathematician told me that before he started a marathon race, that most physical of all the athletic programme, he would set himself a mathematical problem that would need some three hours of mental grappling for a solution to be found. In this way he ensured that he wouldn't become bored with the limited pattern of activity that distance running presents. In this way he made the twenty-six-mile race into a complete activity occupying the mind as well as the body.

Such a character, who loved running but needed to strengthen his intention by mental gymnastics, would have been a 'natural' for the sport of orienteering. Here he would have found the complete absorption of the mind while the body revels in the best and most natural exercise of all—that of running. Cocooned in an aura of utter concentration the orienteer meanders, albeit like a river in flood, across, over and through some of the best of the wonderful countryside in Britain. To the best of his physical ability, the orienteer navigates from defined point to defined point, permutating and computing all the exact knowledge and information available from the Ordnance Survey map. For some two hours the mind rationalizes the body's progress—a complete experience and a formula for happiness.

It is like a car rally but done on foot with the one individual being the driver, navigator and providing the power-output as well.

Orienteering with its juxtaposition of mental awareness and athletic fitness provides the ideal recreation for all those who prefer the muscular mill to be oiled by skill and technical ability. The numbers of those taking part in competitions is growing rapidly. More and more young and not so young men and women are finding that a map and compass, together with the stop-watch and the spur of competition, make a far better excuse for a strenuous run or an enjoyable ramble than does owning a dog!

Although comparatively new in this country the sport of orienteering has been practised in Sweden, where it originated, since 1918. Like many others of the more modern sports that have become world-wide during the past twenty-five years, orienteering was invented to provide an answer to a particular problem. In the same way as volley-ball and basket-ball were thought up to provide the answer to what to do with the not-so-active in a limited space, orienteering was started to encourage young people to make use of the forest for physical and mental enjoyment. It was a Major Killander, a Swedish Youth and Scout leader, who, noticing a fall-off in the number of participants in track and field athletics, decided to use the natural environment of the Swedish countryside to try and encourage active participation in running again. To make his 'running projects' more appealing he set courses in the forest and issued maps and compasses to the competitors. His prototype events were enormously successful and he was encouraged to extend his ideas further.

Ernst Killander, the 'father of orienteering' spread his gospel well, and in 1922 the first District Championship was held. In these early days of Swedish orienteering the courses were quite easy with the controls set on large features. This was because Swedish maps at that time were unreliable, being picturesque rather than cartographic. By the mid-1930's the maps had greatly improved and so the quality of the map-reading aspect of orienteering advanced too. Previously a skier or good track runner had been able to win comfortably in orienteering events, but now with the coming of more precise controls, it was the complete orienteer who won the big events, not just the fit athlete.

Orienteering was a democratic sport from the start, little or no specialist equipment was required to be able to compete. Competitors were just told to 'come as you like'. And they did, in cast-off clothes and old shoes.

By 1935 the sport had spread throughout Sweden and a national organization was formed to co-ordinate the activity. In 1937 the first national championships was held and about 100 senior men qualified for the race. In 1938 the Swedish Orienteering Association (Svenska Orienteringsförbundet—SOFT) took over the sport for all 'foot' races, while orienteering on skis was catered for by the national ski association.

SOFT found that it had a proverbial tiger by the tail and it wasn't long before the sport became an integral part of Swedish life. Competitions ranged from élite cross-country-type races in the desolate forest regions to family week-end excursions around the woods close to Stockholm. Recently, in 1963, a promotional contest in Sweden involved 182,000 people, or about one in every twenty of the entire population. There are now 1,270 clubs affiliated to the SOFT with some 25,000 active adult members including about 3,000 women. In 1963 there were 217 big national competitions, 24 Nordic races (involving teams from Sweden, Norway and Finland) and 7 international meetings.

The largest event on the annual fixture list is the 100 km. Relay Race. This inter-club event over about 65 miles is held in the Stockholm area. Each member of the team of ten runners has a 3–9-mile leg to circumnavigate. The race starts on Saturday afternoon and doesn't finish until Sunday morning. Usually about 170 clubs enter for this event, so there are 1,700 con-

ORIENTEERING

testants involved. There can be few other sports in the world which can claim such mass participation.

The Swedish government were not long in recognizing that this activity was not only valuable from a point of view of health, but that it provided a basis of practical geography as well. Consequently, orienteering has been a compulsory subject in Swedish schools since 1942. It is introduced into the curriculum for the 9–10-years-old child, where he learns first about maps and scale. At the age of 14 the children compete for a special orienteering proficiency badge. This test not only includes solving map-reading problems and practical exercises but also questions on forest conservation and nature lore.

That which fulfilled a need and served a purpose in Sweden was obviously designed to prosper in the rest of Scandinavia. Orienteering is also truly a national game in both of Sweden's neighbours, Norway and Finland. There are annual Nordic championship events for both senior and junior men's and women's teams.

In 1961, the International Orienteering Federation was established at a meeting in Copenhagen. By 1964, eleven countries had affiliated to the IOF; Bulgaria, Denmark, Czechoslovakia, West Germany, East Germany, Finland, Norway, Hungary, Austria, Switzerland and Sweden.

The first European Championship was held in Norway in 1962, and the host country also provided the winner of the men's event—Magne Lysfad, a forestry worker. The women's race was won by the blonde Swedish girl Ulla Lindkvist. These championships are held every two years and the 1964 event was held in the forests above Lausanne. This time the Swiss showed that fifteen years of orienteering experience was enough to provide a champion and although the men's race was won by a Finn, Erkki Kohvakka, the women's race was convincingly won by Margrit Thommen from Geneva.

In 1962, the Swedes decided to extend their 'colonization' to Britain, and Baron 'Rak' Lagerfelt, of the Stockholm Orienteering Club came across to attempt a transplant. His obvious choice of a fertile soil was in Scotland, as the environment was in many areas similar to Sweden.

ORIENTEERING

The Scots were already outdoor-orientated and had through the Scottish Tourist Board been developing both ski-ing and pony trekking as recreational pursuits. They quickly saw the possibilities offered by orienteering and offered complete co-operation to Baron Lagerfelt through the services of the Scottish Council of Physical Recreation. A comprehensive programme of training courses was soon started with the annual championship being the focal point of the year's activity.

The first Championship was held in May 1962 at Dunkeld, in the Tay valley, Perthshire, and the Scottish Orienteering Association was formed at the same meeting. Since those early days the Association has concerned itself with a massive training scheme and organizing a system of District Committees. There is little doubt that the sport will become truly widespread north of the Border.

South of the Border the explosion of orienteering on to the sporting scene appears to be the logical conclusion to ten or so years of encroachment that the stop-watch has made into the British hills and moorlands. In fact, ever since the 'Great Race' chapter of Thomas Firbank's book *I Bought a Mountain*, attracted attention to the circuit of the Welsh 3,000-ft. mountains, there has been a growing enthusiastic group of tough young men who delight in setting records for ascents and circuits of mountain peaks and moorlands. These hardy performers have lived in a fringe world between athletics and mountaineering—one weekend would find them under the jurisdiction of the Amateur Athletic Association's rules running on the track or across the country, while the following week sees them under the stars in a tent and involved in racing across the peat hags of Derbyshire or climbing at speed up and down the 4,000-ft. screes of Ben Nevis.

They were enjoying the informality of the out-of-doors and responding actively to the spur of competition. These men soon found that orienteering provided the ideal outlet for their energies and they were to provide the nucleus of English Orienteering.

The case of England's first orienteering club, the South Ribble Orienteering Club, makes just this point. This club started life as an enthusiastic band of mountaineers centred on Preston in Lancashire. In 1962 they formed themselves into a voluntary mountain rescue team, the South Ribble Search and Rescue Team. The driving force behind the team was a climber called Gerry Charnley from Liverpool, and it was he who first involved the group in the manning of check points for various mountain races in the north of England. For Gerry Charnley also had a foot in the runners' camp as he was a member of the Clayton-le-Moors Harriers, so bit by bit he steered members of both clubs towards the existing fell races.

In 1963, he persuaded a team from his running club to enter for the second Scottish National Orienteering Championship and to everyone's surprise, except Gerry's, Clayton-le-Moors won the senior men's team competition. This success encouraged him to run an orienteering event at Whitewell, near Clitheroe, and this time he involved both of his groups in the race. The South Ribble Search and Rescue Team arranged for the manning of the control points and the Harriers provided most of the competitors. By the following year, 1964, the searchers and rescuers were convinced that they were missing some fun in life, so they changed their name to the South Ribble Orienteering Club and began looking for competition. Thus it was that the first English Orienteering Club was formed.

Moving into full-time orienteering from the other direction was the Clayton-le-Moors Harriers. This club had long been acknowledged as a group which included 'mountain goats' in its membership list. They had many successes and had been foremost in the pioneering of such races as the Lake District Mountain Trial, premier fell races such as Ben Nevis, Goat Fell and Cairngorm and for many years, since in fact 1956, had organized the annual Three Peaks Race which traverses the summits of Ingleborough, Pen-y-Ghent and Wernside.

By the end of 1965 many of its members found that they had divided loyalties and to avoid schizophrenia a new club was set up, the Pendle Forest Orienteers, to serve the interests of those who were putting the sport of orienteering first in their lives.

Although only some fifteen months had elapsed between the forming of England's first orienteering club and the establishment of the Pendle Foresters, this last named club was barely to get into the first dozen English orienteering clubs, for things had been stirring south of the Thames in the woods of Surrey. In January 1965, a Surrey Education Committee Course on orienteering was strongly supported by men and women teachers in the county, almost at once current and ex-international runners were caught in the excitement of the 'new' game. Such names as Dr. Roger Bannister, Christopher Brasher, Gordon Pirie, Martin Hyman and Bruce Tulloh appeared on the results sheet, but to the teachers' surprise the big names didn't hit the top-ten overnight.

It was the fable of the Hare and the Tortoise in modern dress. Clutching at their maps, carrying their compasses like St. Christopher charms around their necks, the trained athletes bounded off from the starting line down the first available path and hoped by sheer running ability to visit all the controls in the forest during their rapid if erratic progress. Interspersed among them from the more academic world were the professional geographers, youth hostellers, scouts, and fell walkers. This group stepped confidently, if diffidently to the start. Once with the maps in their hands they quickly took grid bearings, converted them to magnetic readings and set off through the trees. The pattern of success was fairly predictable and went like this in the early days of races in Surrey. Initial success went first to the clever, and the first race was won by a schoolboy fresh from GCE geography at his Walton-on-Thames school. In the same race Gordon Pirie, maybe not quite so fit as in his old record-making 5,000 metre days of the mid-50's, but still in good condition, failed to finish. For nearly two hours he raced backwards and forwards across the Hurt Woods, near Peaslake. After this time he had found only one control, and that by chance, of the six that were in the few square miles of forest and sandstone ridge. Eventually he had to knock on an old lady's door and ask his way back from her cottage to the village school where he had started from.

However, this is only half the story. A month and two races later the schoolboy, Graham Westbrook, was struggling to get into the first ten finishers, while Gordon Pirie—home-work done and manipulating his 'Silva' compass with élan—had moved to second place in a field of sixty.

This incident, and many other similar ones, indicate the basic pattern that orienteering adopts when introduced into a community. First, the tortoises win comfortably with the hares leaping all over the countryside from hill to hill finding the red and white banners only by chance. Then the hares go away and do some studying and begin to run most of the time in the right direction, to record better times than the tortoises. Finally, deprived of the taste of honey that early success has given them, the tortoises shrug off their shells and start to go out running-training.

Hence the cycle is complete and now the orienteering community allows success to go to those who are both clever and fast, skilful with map and compass and fit in the lungs and legs.

It is somewhat surprising that a sport that has so many qualities admired by the British took so long to get established in this country. Two reasons have contributed to this lapse. The first was the lack of suitable cheap maps, for although we have the finest Ordnance Survey maps in the world, their cost was usually prohibitive to the would-be orienteering organizer. The most often seen and used One-Inch to the Mile map is not suitable for normal orienteering purposes, mainly because there isn't enough detail either to set a course or to estimate progress when competing. Consequently, it is the larger scale 1:25,000 (about $2\frac{1}{2}$ inches to the mile) series of Ordnance Survey maps that are most widely used for the sport. Unfortunately, these beautifully produced maps are relatively expensive in terms of area of ground represented on each sheet, and it might easily mean that for any one competition two 5s. 6d. maps might be necessary. It was obvious that a sport that involved the novice in an outlay of over 10s. a race had little chance of becoming popular. Luckily for orienteering, cheap copying processes finally made it possible to supply to the competitor an excellent black and white reproduction of the area of the map needed for well under a shilling a copy.

The second reason for a certain tardiness in the development of the sport in England was the completely unfounded view that the English countryside did not have enough in-built challenge readily available. This 'inferiority complex' was particularly evident in the attitude of the orienteers in the early events in Surrey. We knew from the four or five events organized in the early part of 1965 that we possessed terrain that was difficult and enjoyable, but at the back of our minds we were convinced that Gerry Charnley and his Northern boys must have at their doorstep much better areas to race across and through. By May 1965 members of the Southern Navigators and the Occasional Orienteers decided to establish the Southern place in the orienteering pecking order. They invited Clayton-le-Moors Harriers and the South Ribble teams down for a race in the Surrey woods beneath Leith Hill. Because they had no yardstick either to judge their own talents or to assess the quality of the beech and fir forests of Surrey it was a critical day for the development of the sport in the south.

In fact, the race organizer was even worried in case the Northerners trampled through the course and disappeared back up the M 1 before any domestic competitor reached the second control. He need not have worried.

The deceptive looking silver-birch and beech quietly swallowed up both the Clayton-le-Moors and the South Ribble teams, and masticated them thoroughly for nearly two hours before spitting them out. They returned to Lancashire muttering, 'If only we had country like this up North'. Obviously, the lowland forests and heaths of England had just as much to offer, if not more, than the wilder parts of the country. Incidentally, this race, the toughest held up to that time in England, was won by Bruce Tulloh, with Occasional Orienteer team-mate Martin Hyman eight minutes behind in second place. Both these international distance runners had taken about ninety minutes to cover the under-7-mile course. The team event was won by the Southern Navigators' Club.

This outburst of activity in the South was echoed by races held in North Wales, the Peak District and in the West Midlands. The problem of co-ordination on a national scale became evident and in October 1965 the English Orienteering Association was founded. A working committee was elected from all the regions of England where the sport was practised and it was asked to prepare a constitution, rules, and regulations of competition.

Under the chairmanship of Olympic Gold-medallist Christopher Brasher, meetings were held to consider the translated copies of the Swedish and Norwegian rules. With due consideration to the English environment all that was best in the two documents was incorporated into the English Association's rules.

One important aspect of the rules was concerned with the sport's attitude to 'amateurism'. Internationally the sport makes no differentiation between those who might be designated amateur or professional in other games, and orienteering calls all of its adherents competitors. Anyone can enter an orienteering race; the professional footballer, the Grasmere Sports fell-runner and the amateur athlete can all race together. As there are no money prizes allowed in orienteering, there is little likelihood that any amateur association will object to its members indulging in this game as well. The Honorary Secretary of the Amateur Athletic Association has made the position quite clear as it affects his sport in the following letter:

C. Brasher, Esq.,   *16th July, 1965.*
Chairman of the
English Orienteering Association.

Dear Mr. Brasher,

You may recall that you spoke to me at Windsor where we were gathered for the start of the Polytechnic Marathon on the subject of Orienteering. I have had a word with Harold Abrahams in this connection and since he confirmed the view I have reached I can now say to you with confidence that amateur athletes can compete against whom they choose in this sport without endangering their amateur status as far as we are concerned, provided always that there is no question of competing for money prizes.

All good wishes.

Yours sincerely,
(*Signed*) BARRY WILLIS
Honorary Secretary.

ORIENTEERING

All the regulations were agreed upon at the 1966 Annual General Meeting of the Association held in conjunction with the 1st English Championships, which took place at Hindhead, Surrey, in May. They are all published elsewhere in this book.

During this period application was also made by the E.O.A to join the International Orienteering Federation, and England became the fourteenth member nation, and was able to send a team to the 1st World Championships held in Finland in October 1966.

The ground was now prepared for the amalgamation of the English and Scottish Associations and the subsequent rationalization of the Rules of Competition and Control Terminology in the U.K. Successful negotiations took place between the two sets of officials throughout the early part of 1967 and a provisional constitution was prepared for presentation at a General Meeting held the night before the National Championships. The motion to form a British Orienteering Federation was carried, and the race the next morning in the Hamsterly Forest, County Durham, became the first British Championship.

Orienteering is now taking its place as a growing tree in the garden of British Sport. The British Orienteering Federation working through the Scottish Orienteering Association and the nine Regional Associations in England and Wales is putting roots down into the fertile soil of school and youth activity. The Services, too, are aware of the attractions of the sport and are actively promoting orienteering. Coverage is well spread and comprehensive.

In 1949, Geoffrey Dyson, the Chief National Coach to the Amateur Athletic Association, came back from Sweden where he had been visiting Gösta Holmer, the Swedish National Coach. Holmer told him that the future success of middle distance running in Sweden was being threatened by a young sport called orienteering—and this within a year of the Swedish athletes' many triumphs on the track at the 1948 Olympics. Holmer went on to explain that the young men seemed to prefer to run through the forests rather than around a track.

Orienteering may never reach such a height of popularity in this country, but it will, without a doubt, become a valuable and appreciated part of the British recreational scene.

2

Getting Started

Nothing could be simpler than getting into your first orienteering race—you will need very little equipment; only your enthusiasm and some old clothes are necessary. An entry into a race is obtained by writing to any of the various secretaries who control the Regional Associations. You will then be sent a fixture list and the names and addresses of all the established orienteering clubs in the area you live.

The pattern of communication then goes like this, and perhaps the best way to illustrate the procedure is to reproduce the details connected with an actual race which took place. The first letter you get from the Regional secretary will contain the fixture list (*see* pages 27–29).

As you will see from this list there are many different standards of event as well as different methods of orienteering. Naturally enough, the novice competitor will be attracted to the easier events, such as No. 3 on the List. Here we know that the total distance of the course is fairly short—just over four miles, and that the going under foot is not too tough.

These novices' events are usually designed so that everyone is encouraged by their experience. The organizer makes a course which starts very easily and progresses to a mild sting in the tail. Consequently, everyone finds the first couple of markers, which are usually set at an obvious path junction, and the clever novice is also extended by the last control or so which is placed on a feature that is not so easily found such as a minor spur or ring-contour. Everyone goes home happy, understanding that there is more to this sport of orienteering than they first thought.

ORIENTEERING

T H E   S O U T H E R N   Ó R I E N T E E R I N G
A S S O C I A T I O N

FINAL FIXTURE LIST - AUTUMN 1965

1. SEPTEMBER 12th

   The Lake District Mountain Trial

   This annual event is always well supported by the northern lads
   and it provides one of the best days out in the Hills of the
   year. The event is a severe test of route finding ability and
   involves some 15-20 miles of traversing of the Central Fells.
   All entries must be from persons over 21 years old.

   Venue: Traveller's Rest Inn, Grasmere
   First man away: 10 a.m.
   Entry Fee: 5/-
   Entries: By August 9th. to Gerry Charnley,
                               9 St. Stephen's Road,
                               Hightown, Nr. Liverpool

   A strong party from Ranelagh Harriers, led by Jeff Bull, is
   travelling North on Saturday, September 11th. Otherwise the
   only entry we know of from the South is from Chris Brasher
   (who will probably be leaving London at 6.0 a.m. on Sunday,
   September 12th). He has space in his car and might be able
   to arrange late entries. (RIChmond 8822)

2. SEPTEMBER 18th

   A "Night Event" by the Occasional Orienteers.

   An Open event - Seniors, juniors and women - Team and Individual entries.

   Venue: Elstead Junior School (903433) near Godalming.
   First man away: 8 p.m.
   Course: Under 5 miles
   Entry fee: 2/6d. Seniors. 1/- Juniors (under 19 on the day
                                                of the race)
   Entries: To Martin Hyman, 2 Barn Court, Elstead, Surrey.

3. OCTOBER 3rd

   A Novices' Event (Organised by the Southern Navigators')

   An Open event designed for those competitors who are still
   finding life a bit confusing in the major events.

   Venue: In the Dorking area. The actual starting point will
             be revealed one week before the competition.
   Course: 4-5 miles in fairly easy terrain.
   First man away: 11 a.m.
   Entry Fee: Seniors 2/6d. Juniors 1/0
   Entries: By September 27th. To Peter Palmer,
                               c/o Rydens School,
                               Hersham Road,
                               Walton-on-Thames, Surrey.

ORIENTEERING

4. OCTOBER 17th

An Experts' Event (Organised by the Southern Navigators')

An Open event - Seniors, Juniors and Women - Team and Individual entries.
This competition will be similar in character to the 'tough' Coldharbour event of last May. Controls will be placed in situations where skill will be needed to locate them successfully.

Venue: In mid-Surrey. The actual starting point will be
        sent to all applicants in the week before the race.
First man away: 10.30 a.m.
Course: 7 miles of the roughest terrain available.
Entry fee: 2/6d. Seniors. 1/- Juniors (only experienced
                                       juniors should enter)

Entries: By October 9th. to John Disley,
                        38 Broom Close,
                        Teddington, Middlesex

This will be a team event as far as possible. There will be an invasion from other areas so let's put out as many teams as possible.
For those in the Morden/Mitcham/Croydon areas, there is the North Downs Orienteers (Sec. Geoffrey Wood, 161 St. Helier Avenue, Morden, Surrey). For those in Richmond/Kingston and SW London areas, there is the Southern Navigators' Club (Sec. Chris Brasher, The Navigator's House, River Lane, Petersham, Surrey). Don't be shy about writing and asking to join (enclose a s.a.e. please) and say whether you are an expert, a novice, a junior (under 19 on the day of the event) or just plain average. Each club can enter as many different teams as it likes.
Those living in other areas might think of starting a club. If you are prepared to act as temporary secretary, write to John Disley and he will put you in touch with any other competitors from your area.

OCTOBER 23rd - 24th

The 1965 Scottish Championships

Although the great distance to travel may reduce the enchantment of a quick belt through the Trossachs or whatever area the organisers choose for the race, we still hope that a team or two from the south will make the journey. With full cars and camping the cost of the trip should not be more than a fiver, and that includes a contingent sum for strong drink. The south should be well represented in this race and now is the time to start saving pennies and acquiring skill and fitness. Those interested should contact Chris Brasher,
                            The Navigator's House,
                            River Lane,
                            Petersham, Surrey

ORIENTEERING

6. <u>OCTOBER 31st Sunday</u>

<u>Open Championship Meeting - SHROPSHIRE</u>

Organiser: Alan Batstone,
              Chairman West Midlands Orienteering Association,
              Bournville College of Further Education,
              The Green,
              Bournville, Birmingham 30

Overnight accomodation on Saturday and meals available.
After this event a meeting will be held to form an English
Orienteering Association.
The Southern Navigators will certainly send a team so if you
are interested please write to Chris Brasher (address under
event 7). He will enter the team and co-ordinate transport
so please say whether you have any spare places or need transport and also whether you intend going up Saturday or Sunday
morning.

7. <u>NOVEMBER 14th</u>

<u>An Orienteering Event</u> - (Organised by the Southern Navigators)

An Open event - Seniors, Juniors and Women - Team and indivi-
                 dual entries.
Venue: In the Dorking Area. The actual starting point will be
       sent to all applicants in the week preceding the race.
First man away: 10.30 a.m.
Course: 5 to 6 miles (not too difficult)
Entry fee: Seniors 2/6d. Juniors 1/-
Entries: By November 5th. to Bill Hill,
                              81 St. Leonards Road,
                              East Sheen, S.W.14

8. <u>NOVEMBER 27th</u>

<u>A Night Orienteering Event</u> - (Organised by the Southern
                                         Navigators)

An open cross-country competition for Seniors,
Juniors and Women - Team and individual entries.

Venue: In the Richmond environs.
First man away: 6.30 p.m.
Course: 3 miles
Entry fee: Seniors 2/6d. Juniors 1/-
Entries: By November 20th to Chris Brasher (address as under 7)

9. <u>DECEMBER 12th</u>

<u>A score Orienteering Event</u>

The idea in a Score Event is to collect as many controls as possible in the time limit (usually 90 mins) set by the organiser
(Organised by the Occasional Orienteers)

Venue: At Borden Camp, six miles south of Farnham
First man away: 10 a.m.
Course: Depends upon how fast you can run in the time, few
        average more than 6 m.p.h.
Entry fee: Seniors 2/6d. Juniors 1/-
Entries: By December 4th, to Martin Hyman, 2 Barn Court, Elstead
                                                         Surrey.

<u>August 28th 1965</u>

Chairman, S.O.A.   Hon Sec. S.O.A.
C.W.Brasher, Esq.,   J.I.Disley, Esq.,
The Navigator's House,   38 Broom Close, Teddington,
River Lane,   Middlesex
Petersham, Surrey

ORIENTEERING

No sport can expect to develop unless it extends a continuous challenge to the performer—always a little more to be learned, usually from mistakes made, always a new way to be tried of being more efficient and successful. Orienteering can provide a constant challenge to the wits.

In any case, the beginner will be in good company in a novices' race, for the only people allowed to enter are those who have never finished in the first twenty of an Open race and the field will contain many who have never competed before. A letter to the organizer will gain an entry for you, but you should enclose a stamped, addressed envelope with your application.

Unless the organizer acknowledges your entry at once, you should not expect to hear from him until several days before the date of the competition, for the actual venue for the event needs to be kept secret until as near the day of the race as possible. In this way the organizer tries to make sure that the area is a strange place for everyone. Pre-race-day practice over an area likely to be used for a race is to be discouraged.

A couple of days before the event the organizer will send out further details of his event to all who have entered. The letter will look like the one opposite.

So the great day dawns of your first competition—and you may well be involved in an early start with the dawn. The venue is known to you and you have your starting-time. Many starting-points, based as they often are in the heart of rough country, are not readily accessible by public transport. It may well be necessary either to arrange a lift in a car or to allow a generous margin of time for a walk from the nearest rail-head or bus stop to the start.

Your letter from the organizer indicated that changing facilities will be primitive, so that some thought will need to be given to arriving half-changed or being prepared to change in the back of a car or behind a bush.

Most beginners will find that a pair of old flannels or track-suit trousers together with a shirt and long-sleeve jersey will provide adequate protection against the weather and the abrasive qualities of gorse, bracken and tree branches. On the feet a pair of light boots, climbing, hockey or even soccer boots are suitable, while strong gym shoes will suffice if the ground is dry.

ORIENTEERING

THE SOUTHERN NAVIGATORS

NOVICES' EVENT—*Sunday, October 3rd*

Information Sheet

1. *Venue.* Mickleham Village School (173537—O.S. 170). The school is off the main A.24 road.
2. *Car Parking.* Is available in the school playground.
3. *Changing Facilities.* These are rather limited, and you are advised to come ready to compete. However, the girls will be able to change in a classroom.
4. *Start Time.* Please report to the reception desk between :—

$$10.15 - 10.30 \ a.m.$$

5. *The Course.* There will be some areas of the course where brambles and bracken will make long pants desirable. If shorts are worn it should be in conjunction with long stockings. By the best route around the course the distance is 4⅓ miles.
6. *Private Property.* High fences make it obvious where the border of 'common' land and private property comes. Please go around all such land and also fields under cultivation.
7. *All competitors must report back to the* FINISH—*whether they complete the course or not. We don't want to search for you!*
8. Enjoy yourself and good luck.

As you get more experienced you will soon become more sophisticated about your gear, and this book will indicate possible trends later in its pages.

You will also need a compass, unless the organizer has indicated that he can lend, hire or sell you this item of equipment. The ordinary 'watch-type' compass has its limitations, as you will soon find out during the race. So also has the expensive prismatic compass. You will probably find that most of your fellow competitors will be using a 'protractor-type' instrument —more of this later.

ORIENTEERING

The only other pieces of equipment you require to take with you will be a red ball-point pen and a stiffish plastic bag to enclose your map.

As you travel the last half a mile or so to the venue you will probably see several intent figures either running purposefully down a side lane, or paused standing facing the forest with their heads bent low over a map. These are the early starters already 'lost' in the involvement of the activity and oblivious to your apprehensive gaze.

There are several different methods of 'processing' your participation, but basically, after you have reported your presence, you will find yourself in possession of a map, and a competitor's card. In this pre-off period you can take the opportunity to get yourself organized—everyone around you will seem to be busy, so what is there to do?

Obviously, now is the time to check that you have the compass, pen and plastic bag; it is also an excellent time to study the map and read the instructions that often accompany the map on the sheet. You will at once notice that the map is not the genuine article, it is a black and white copy of the Ordnance Survey 1 : 25,000 map, often with added features marked on it and some notes in the margin.

NOTES TO COMPETITORS

Scale of Map is $2\frac{1}{2}$ inches to the Mile.
Magnetic Variation is 8° 20′ West of North.
    The Representation on this Map of a track or foot-path is no evidence of a Right of Way.
Avoid Trespassing on Private Property.
Rivers and Streams are represented thus:
Ponds and Lakes thus:
Controls are marked by Red and White banners.
Controls must be Visited in the order indicated on the Master-Map.

Reproduced from the Ordnance Survey map with the sanction of the Controller of H.M. Stationery Office, Crown Copyright reserved.

ORIENTEERING

These instructions will vary from race to race, but they are always extremely important and often the organizer's only way of conveying special orders of the day to the competitor.

If you have only been used to the more ubiquitous 1 in. to the mile map, the larger scale of the 1:25,000 map will take some getting used to, at least in your first race. The grid lines are still there and are still the same kilometre apart so that it is possible to quickly appreciate that things happen much more frequently on this scale of map. The detail is expanded to include such features as field boundaries, wells, and even the smallest farm buildings. The lack of differentiating colours makes it a little difficult at first to distinguish between a contour line and a feature, but it is amazing how quickly the eye learns to sort out the different shades of black and give meaning to the mass of lines. (*See* Map 7.)

Together with the map you will have received the Control card. It will probably look like this:

NAME					TEAM
CLASS					FINISH TIME
Controls					START TIME
1	2	3	4	5	TIME TAKEN
6	7	8	9	10	POSITION

This card will already have your name recorded on it and also the Start Time. When the Starter calls out your start time, in this case 10:41.00, he will give you one further piece of paper and direct you into the Master Map room or area. The piece of paper will be your list of Controls and will look like the table on page thirty-four.

ORIENTEERING

No.	Map. Ref.	Description of Control
1	179535	The Trig. Point.
2	177529	The path fork.
3	175523	The hair-pin bend on the road.
4	173514	The foot-bridge.
5	181510	The junction of paths.
6	187514	The corner of the field.
7	186520	The crossing of the track and the path.
8	184530	An iron gate across the track.
9	184535	On the path.
10	173537	The school.

The figures 1 to 10 indicate the order of the Controls—they in fact prescribe the 'course'. The six-figure Map Reference is a device for directing your attention to a square hundred metres of the map. This technique is explained in Chapter 3. The description of the Control is self-explanatory, except in that when the organizer uses the definite article, 'the', he indicates that the feature is not only on the ground but also marked on the map. In this case above, No. 8 Control shows that an iron gate—with the indefinite article—is not indicated as such on the map.

From the moment you enter the Master Map section, whether it be a room in a village school or an area of the forest where the marked maps are displayed, you are 'Off'. From that second onwards the watch-ticks are all counting and inefficiency on your behalf all adds seconds, minutes or even hours towards your total elapsed time.

As in many other competitive sports, there are times in orienteering when it is best to make haste slowly; in front of the Master-maps is just one of these times. All that is necessary is for the competitor to reproduce on his map several red circles that are indicated on the master-map. The organizer has gone to some lengths to make sure that he has marked every Control precisely by a small circle, and it is well worth the competitor's time and trouble to check and double check that he has reproduced these marks faithfully. The organizer will have also joined together the circles with red lines, and this line together with the number given to each red circle will indicate the correct sequence of the course. The competitor should also number the circles and join them together with a line. While I am at this job I also mark in some large arrow-heads on my map to indicate where North is situated. A fatigued brain, panting body and sweat-filled eyes need every device possible to make interpretation of a map easy. These *aides-mémoire* take only seconds to do but can easily save you many minutes in helping to avoid wrong decisions in the course of the race.

Having added all these additional data to your map, and done it in red ball-point pen for clarity, the map should be put away in some form of protective covering. The cheapest form of cover is a plastic bag and you will probably find this form of protection against rain or even perhaps sweat quite suitable in your early races. However, experienced competitors like to have a stiffer plastic cover and use 'file document' holders which are available in foolscap size. You will also have two other pieces of paper—the route card and the control card; both these should also be kept in the 'map-case'.

You are now ready to move-off, and the great wide world awaits your entrance into orienteering circles. Your skill at cor-relating what you recognize on the ground with the marks on the map, together with your fitness, are now your sole assets. Most novice events are set out in a manner to encourage the first-timer to come again, so that Controls will be sited in fairly obvious places, like at the junction of paths or on the summit of a small hill. All it remains for you to do as a competitor is to find the right path to follow and the right hill to climb. You will be in good company for about two hours as you perambulate around four or five miles of woodlands.

Before long you will come across other 'runners' who, like yourself, have become 'walkers'. All of you will quickly have appreciated that to 'run' a mistake is a very poor investment of energy indeed. In the beginning, it is of course, much easier to pick off land-marks at walking speed, and a false move can usually be detected after just a couple of hundred yards. Now and again you will come across small groups of puzzled people twisting their maps in their hands and tapping their compasses as if they were barometers. You may be feeling insecure yourself and gladly join their company feeling that three or four heads are better than one. The only advice I can give you here is to say that seldom are corporate decisions better than your own individual solution. In fact, one of the biggest problems of the orienteer is to remain aloof, neither seeking or giving advice to fellow competitors. Such a situation will undoubtedly arise in your first race.

As you stride confidently through the trees following what you earnestly believe to be the correct track to the next Control you will suddenly see another, equally confident, runner moving at right angles to your path. Now you will experience the spice of orienteering. Can you be wrong and he right? Do you abandon your intended route and switch to his or do you press on regardless?

Whatever the outcome of your decision on this occasion, the next time you meet the problem it will still be a traumatic moment of truth.

Your correct progress around the course is established by a marking routine at each control. All controls are marked by banners which are red canvas flag or box-kite shapes. They are usually about two feet square and have a white diagonal flash across them. Most organizers display a marker at the start, so that everyone knows for what they are searching.

The markers are never hidden away under a bush or down a hole in the ground. Orienteering is not a treasure hunt but a game of skill, so the markers are hung out for all to see—as long as you are within 25–30 yards of the control. The spirit of the game demands that if the competitor has navigated himself to within a few yards of the right spot, then just normal eyesight will enable the banner to be seen. Indeed, should the placing of the control have to be in thick foliage, then the organizer will often festoon neighbouring branches with red streamers. Orienteering is not a game of chance but a game of skill.

Your presence at a control is proved by marking your control card in the correct little box. The flags usually have a letter painted on them in bold type and this letter is copied on to the card. However, most organizers have a set of self-inking markers which they use to facilitate proof of progress. These small stamps are suspended from the banner by a piece of string and all the competitor has to do is to stamp the card to prove that the control has been visited. In the bigger races, such as a championship, a marshal may also note the progress of the competitor through a control.

The intense satisfaction of finding a red and white marker exactly where you expected it to be is a delight that has to be experienced to be believed. The anticipation is acute as you push through the high bracken to the crest of the ridge. There beneath your feet is the small valley you expected to see, you hear the splash of water and know the stream marked on the map is also present; a quick glance along the stream and there is the foot-bridge and on it a red and white marker. Sheer joy!

Having circumnavigated the course successfully and filled in all the available 'boxes' on the competitor's card, the finish will be reached. Here your finish time is recorded, your card examined and, after all the results are in, you will be given a position. The competitor with the smallest elapsed time is the winner, provided, of course, he visited all the controls in the correct order.

However, if things have gone badly in the thick of the woods and controls have remained hidden from your view, you still must report back to the finish. In many races the organizer gives a clear indication when he is going to start collecting in the control markers and also when he intends to close the final control. Three to four hours is usually enough time for most people to exercise themselves and they should then remember the orienteer's first commandment—'All competitors must report to the Finish whether they have completed the course or not'. This concept of good social behaviour needs to be emphasized at every opportunity. No one objects to turning out for a search party, but everyone has a right to be very annoyed indeed if the object of their search is already on his way home and has just omitted to tell any official that he has retired.

In any case, the post-mortems held at the finish are a most enjoyable part of orienteering and should be participated in by everyone. Over a drink of tea or shandy, plausible explanations can be made, excuses concocted and situations explained. Often the course-setter and his helpers will sit in on these 'teach-ins' and at once find themselves on trial if there is a general consensus of opinion that a marker was wrongly placed or badly designated.

As you drink your second cup of tea you will be amazed to find that you had only abstracted about half the available information from the map. It seems that on listening to the conversation around you that there were many features that you hadn't noticed at all. The man next to you talks about a 'field boundary' that pointed directly to the control and how he noticed a bend in a 'power-line' which indicated exactly where control 5 was situated. All this you missed and yet now on looking at the map you see that it is all there and wonder how you could have been so blind an hour ago?

Several of your new friends mention techniques which you have never heard of before. One of them admits to have taken a 'back-bearing' on a railway bridge to establish his position on a lane; another talks of 'aiming-off' to make sure he was 'collected' by a road on his way to control 3. You will soon realize that it wasn't just your inability to keep running for two hours that prevented you from winning your first event—something else was missing as well.

In any case, whatever the result of your first attempt at orienteering, one thing you can be sure will happen—you will want to do better next time. Your one thought as you make your way home after the race will not be a lament for your wet feet, scratched legs or aching lungs but a need to know when is the next event? You will want a chance as soon as possible to put into practice all the new skills that you have learnt today.

3

The Map

'An orienteer is no better than his map,' so say the Nordic pundits. If this is true then the British orienteer has no excuse for not being amongst the best in the world, for the maps produced by Her Majesty's Ordnance Survey are second to none.

Most of us are familiar with the one-inch to the mile O.S. map and have used it often on walking holidays. We are used to taking some 15–20 minutes to walk an inch of the map. We have also got used to the vertical scale too, and recognize a steep slope by the congregation of the contour lines. Three or four of the brown lines close together usually persuade us to walk round them to a lesser gradient. The seven-colour one-inch map is the walkers' and climbers' guide book. The detail shown by the eighty-odd map symbols is sufficient to establish position, prejudge hazards, and it is also large enough in area, about 700 square miles, to cover a week's walking.

The orienteer, however, craves more detail and information than the 1-in. map can offer. He graduates to the next size up in British map production and learns to appreciate the softer salmon tones of the 1:25,000 map. This map offers some $2\frac{1}{2}$ in. of map for every mile on the ground. It is, of course, far more than just two and a half times the area of the 1-in. to the mile map, in fact, it is over six times the area, so the map maker has far more opportunity to depict what exists.

The undulations of the ground are also explained with double the accuracy, for the contour lines on the $2\frac{1}{2}$ in. map are only 25 ft apart.

Although the '$2\frac{1}{2}$ in.' has just half a dozen more symbols to its credit than the '1-in.' map, these additional conventional signs are 'money in the bank' as far as the orienteer is concerned. The extra signs expand 'rough pasture' to show brushwood, furze, heath and moor and include field boundaries, wells and springs. The former symbols give a good indication what the going under-foot is likely to be, although peat hags are still unpredictable, and the latter signs enable controls to be set out with more accuracy.

The '2½-in. map' is made with four colours only—black, grey, blue and orange and is usually about 1¾ ft. × 1½ ft. representing about 40 square miles. In fact, you would need to buy twenty of these sheets to cover the area normally represented by the 1 in. to the mile map. Here at once we are presented with a problem which, until its solution in Britain, held back the sport—the problem was the cost of the map. It was too optimistic to expect a novice to spend at least 5s. 6d. and perhaps 11s. on a map or maps for one race as well as an entry fee. Luckily, with the advent in 1964 of the 'dye-line' copier, good cheap copies of maps became available, and in all but the top championships orienteers use black and white reproductions. These sheets reproduced with the sanction of the Stationery Office (*see* Chapter 8) can be produced for a few pence each.

It is remarkable how soon it is possible to adjust the senses to accepting the monochrome map. At first the contours get muddled up with the lanes and the second class roads all look like railways. Streams, instead of being blue, are now black wiggly lines, for most of the copying processes will not pick up the colour blue too well and, consequently, the streams and lakes have to be inked in before the map is copied.

So the orienteer's working map is for all intents and purposes a monochrome, usually black, copy of the 1 : 25,000 Ordnance Survey map.

New Second Series Map

An exciting new 1 : 25,000 map, the Second Series, is gradually replacing the old series. This map is printed as a double horizontal sheet, depicting two 10-kilometre squares side by side. It will be many years before this edition covers the whole country, but where it is available it offers added advantages to the orienteer. Each double-sheet costs 7s. 6d.

The first improvement over the first series is that all woods and forests are coloured green, instead of grey. The second innovation is the inclusion of a green dotted line which indicates a public right of way on footpaths and bridle ways. This feature, which used to be only printed on the 'definitive' maps, is a very welcome addition to the information needed by the organizer of orienteering races.

Other alterations concern the symbols used for showing vegetation, pits and quarries, and rock features. These symbols are shown in black and white in Maps 8, 9 and 10.

There is no doubt that this new map is the finest in the world at this scale and a great credit to the surveying and printing resources of the Ordnance Survey.

Information on the orienteer's map

Apart from the map itself, the sheet the orienteer is given at the start of a race will probably look like that in Map 1.

There is a certain amount of marginal information:

1. The Occasional Orienteers—Score Event, Bordon, Hants. Sunday, 12th December 1965.
2. Details of the Map this copy was made from: Sheet SU 73. Compiled from 6 in. sheets last fully revised 1913–34. Other partial systematic revision 1938–55 has been used. Reprinted with minor changes 1961.
3. Scale 1: 25,000 or about $2\frac{1}{2}$ in. to 1 mile.
4. Grid line numbers in all margins.
5. A border of black and white marks—each mark represents 100 metres.
6. 'Reproduced from the Ordnance Survey map with the sanction of the Controller of H.M. Stationery Office, Crown Copyright Reserved.'
7. Indication of Magnetic Variation. Grid North at the centre of this sheet is 0° 50′ 02″ E of True North. Magnetic Variation is 08° 30′ W of Grid North for January 1960. Annual Change 10′ E.
8. Not all paths are shown.

9. Not all buildings exist.
10. Restricted areas are fully fenced in.
11. Depiction of Ponds and Streams.
12. The representation on this map of a Road, Track, or Footpath, is no evidence of the existence of a right of way.

Let us take several of the above points and see why the organizer took the trouble to embellish his map area with these further details.

A. *Scale*

Just to be quite sure that there is no doubt in our minds, the Scale of this map is explained to us in four different ways.

1. By a figure, 1: 25,000, this is called a 'representative fraction', and it means that for every unit on the map there are 25,000 of the same unit on the ground.
2. In words. About $2\frac{1}{2}$ Inches to the 1 Mile.
3. By a graphic line scale: 0–1,000 yards and 0–4 furlongs.
4. By a border pattern within the Grid. Each dash is $\frac{1}{10}$th of a Kilometre grid square long.

The orienteer is extremely interested in scale and he is constantly estimating either by the eye, or measuring with some form of rule, how far away the next land-mark is. He is seldom concerned with distances of more than a mile. The orienteer can be likened to the captain of a coastal steamer; both of them only really feel happy when they can see the next identifiable feature. Long passages across featureless areas are to be avoided.

B. *Grids*

Both the 1 in. map and the $2\frac{1}{2}$ in. edition are covered by a lattice-work of solid black lines. These 'grid-lines' are parallel to the borders of the map and are one kilometre apart. They are all part of the National Grid System, which is a location device for the whole of the British Isles. By using the letters and figures attached to the grid system it is possible to pin-point a spot to a square 100 metres.

Although not especially constructed with the game of orienteering in mind, the grid system has given British orienteering a sophistication that few European countries can approach. Instead of having to designate a certain spot on the map by reference to 'so many tenths of an inch south-west of the "e" in "for*est*",' the grid system allows a simple 'six-figure' reference to do the job perfectly.

It will be seen that the vertical lines—called Eastings, are numbered in the top and bottom margins of the map and that the horizontal lines—call Northings, are numbered at the sides of the sheet. These numbers, always quoted in pairs, can be used to designate any individual one of the kilometre squares on the map.

For any square the number of the line that makes its west boundary is quoted first, then the number of the line that makes the lower border of the square. This will give a 'four-figure' map reference and directs attention to a specific one-thousand metre square. (*See* Fig. 1.)

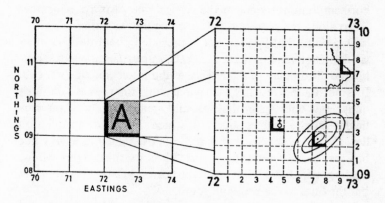

FIGURE 1

Grid lines on the map are at kilometre intervals. The four-figure map reference for square A is 7209.

Square A enlarged
The 100-metre imaginary lines are drawn with dotted lines. The six-figure map references are:

    The church—724093.
    The hill summit—727092.
    The stream bend—729097.

ORIENTEERING

To reduce this area to a square hundred metres, the grid square is divided, in the imagination, into $\frac{1}{10}$ths and this third figure denoting the number of one-tenths across and up is added to the original numbers of the four-figure reference. (*See* Fig. 1.) This is a 'six-figure' map reference.

The most common fault made in calculating six-figure references is to quote the wrong three figures first. On many maps this inversion of the figures will actually produce a place on the map, but it is likely to be many, many miles away from the intended spot. A way to remember which set of figures comes first is to pretend that you are visiting a friend who lives in an apartment in a tall block of flats in a road of blocks of flats. In this case the first number that would concern you as you looked for the right place is the horizontal number along the road. When you had located the foot of the correct block, then you would concern yourself about which floor to climb to in the building. The same system applies to the map—concern yourself with the horizontal numbers before the vertical ones. Always remember —'go along the road first before going up the stairs.'

One point that is often not appreciated about designating a six-figure reference is that exactly the same rules apply to selecting the third figure of a reference as did to picking the first two. It is not the nearest line—imaginary this time—that you must quote, but once again the west and south borders of the particular hundred metre square in which the feature in question lies. (*See* Fig. 2.) So that a spot almost touching a grid line but just to its west will not get '0' as its third figure of the westings trio, but a '9'. It is not the nearest line that is important but the lines to the west and south.

If the '6-inch' map was often used for orienteering, then it would be perfectly possible to use an 'eight-figure' reference system, which would make a reference correct to a ten-metre square.

The orienteer can improve the quality of his 'guess' work in selecting the six-figure by using a 'romer' scale. Certainly, anyone setting a course and designating the position of the controls must use such an instrument.

It is possible to buy a romer from 'car rally equipment' shops, but just as easy to make your own.

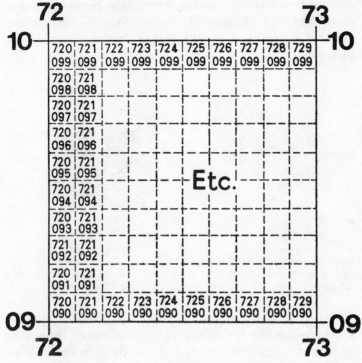

FIGURE 2

Six-figure references in a single Grid square

Any point on the map is designated by the imaginary 100-metre square it lies in, as is shown above.

Design 1. Get a square of thin coloured transparent plastic about 2 in. × 2 in. Using the chequered border of a '2½-in.' map as a guide, mark off on the plastic a square of the grid. With a sharp needle scratch a lattice work of lines joining up the individual 100-metre points to make one hundred small squares. The device can be laid over a grid square on the map and the detail seen clearly through the plastic. It is then quite simple and extremely accurate to ascertain in which 100-metre square the feature in question lies. (*See* Fig. 3.)

Design 2. Again using the black and white border of the map as a guide, mark off the right-angle corner of a piece of stiff card into eleven 100-metre divisions. A postcard-size photograph is very suitable material—use the reverse side. Number the divisions from 1–10, or rather '0', starting from the first mark in from the corner. Cut out the corner 100-metre square. (*See* Figure 3.)

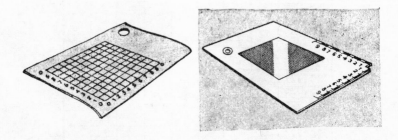

FIGURE 3

Romer—Design 1	*Romer—Design 2*
Made by scratching lines on a piece of coloured transparent plastic.	Made out of a piece of stiff card, with the 'dicing' from the edge of a map making the divisions.

To use, lay the romer parallel to the grid lines so that the feature in question lies within the 'missing' square. Adjust the romer until the division marks are exactly opposite the numbered grid lines and read off the third figures.

C. *Revision Dates*

Maps are only completely up-to-date for a few months. As fast as the cartographer revises his map, along come the builder, farmer and forester to alter the ground yet again. The margin data of an Ordnance Survey map always include the date of the last revision, and the competent race organizer appends the same information to his reproduced sheet. In fact, he has the chance to bring the map completely up-to-date by adding extra detail before the sheet is copied by the machine.

If the margin information tells the orienteer that it is ten years since the last revision took place then he can expect things to be different on the ground from what the map indicates. When a barn or a line of forestry houses is not to be found on the *passé* map, the orienteer does not immediately assume he is lost, but looks to see if the buildings are new enough to have been erected since the map was published.

The same 'second thoughts' apply to unpredicted forest plantations. Actually, coniferous trees grow so quickly that just five years is enough growing time to make what was 'rough pasture' into impassable jungle. Trees also get harvested, but the stumps will then be the evidence that the map-maker knew what he was doing when he drew in all those little Christmas trees on the map.

D. *The Map Symbols*

Apart from explaining to the orienteer that streams are represented by black wavy lines and that ponds are horizontally shaded, the race organizer does not provide any further reference table. The alphabet of the map is the set of conventional signs or map symbols. The cartographer uses over eighty of these symbols to depict various features and tries hard to make it easy for his clientele. Many of the symbols are small drawings of the feature and are hence self-explanatory. In any case a couple of hours homework should enable most people to remember the majority of the signs.

These conventional signs are not printed on the edge of the 2½-in. map, but can be obtained from an official Ordnance Survey agent, price 3d. Most large towns have such an agent.

A monochrome reproduction of these conventional signs is printed as Map 4. The grey/green colour of such symbols as 'Wood, Coniferous, Fenced' comes out grey, while the blue of the estuary, lake and river is barely picked up at all. The orange colour of the contours comes out as black as the original black of the railway. All these slightly tonal variations soon become apparent to the experienced orienteer and he hardly notices the absence of colour.

E. *Contour Lines*

If the roads, rivers, paths and railways make the bones on the map, then the flesh is put on by the contour lines. The orange lines that swirl and twist across the map show the rise and fall, the hummocks and the hollows, and all the undulations of the ground surface. To the orienteer they provide his most reliable source of information. For man-made paths fade away, forests sprout and become lumber, and streams are often seasonal; but the hills and valleys, the spurs and cols are faithful to the map for ever.

Contour lines are imaginary lines which run through places of equal height above mean sea-level at Newlyn, Cornwall. On Ordnance Survey maps the contours are shown as orange lines broken at intervals by numbers which denote their height in feet. On the 1-in. map the contour lines are drawn at intervals of 50 ft., with a thicker line every 250 ft. On the orienteer's 2½-in. map the interval between the contours is 25 ft., with a thicker line every 100 ft. Adding to the overall picture of relief are the 'spot heights', surveyed points which give the exact height of various obvious features, such as the top of a hill, or a col between two peaks. (*See* Fig. 4.)

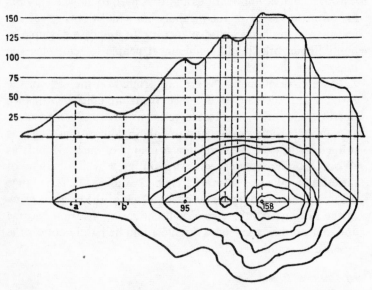

FIGURE 4

The representation of relief by contour lines. Notice how the 25-foot divisions fail to indicate the knoll at 'a' or the 'trough' at 'b'. Spot heights sometimes rectify this omission as at '95' and at the summit.

MAP 1

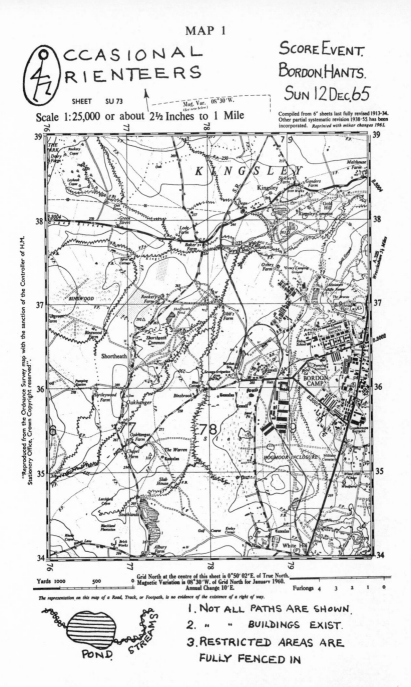

OCCASIONAL ORIENTEERS

SHEET SU 73

Mag. Var. 08°30′W.
(See note below)

Scale 1:25,000 or about 2½ Inches to 1 Mile

SCORE EVENT.
BORDON, HANTS.
SUN 12 DEC. 65

Compiled from 6″ sheets last fully revised 1913-34.
Other partial systematic revision 1938-55 has been
incorporated. *Reprinted with minor changes 1961.*

"Reproduced from the Ordnance Survey map with the sanction of the Controller of H.M. Stationery Office, Crown Copyright reserved".

Yards 1000   500   0

Grid North at the centre of this sheet is 0°50′02″E. of True North.
Magnetic Variation is 08°30′W. of Grid North for January 1960.
Annual Change 10′E.

Furlongs 4   3   2   1   0

The representation on this map of a Road, Track, or Footpath, is no evidence of the existence of a right of way.

POND.   STREAMS.

1. NOT ALL PATHS ARE SHOWN.
2. " " BUILDINGS EXIST.
3. RESTRICTED AREAS ARE
   FULLY FENCED IN

Reduced from foolscap size, the map sheet as produced for
an event at Bordon, Hampshire. The organiser must spend
several hours preparing his master copy, with scissors, glue,
and bits off the margin of an Ordnance Survey map.

MAP 2
Control Terminology and Definition of Features
EXAMPLES FROM 1:25000 MAP

1 The track junction

2 The track crossing

3 The track bend

4 The track end

5 The path junction

6 The path end

7 The path bend

8 The track and the path junction

9 The track and the path crossing

10 The stream source

11 The stream junction

12 The stream bend

13 The lake west corner

14 The pond

15 The outlet

16 The inlet

17 The track and the stream crossing

18 The path and the stream crossing

19 The island

20 The promontory

21 The hill summit

22 The hill summit west ena

23 The hill side

24 The hill foot

25 The hill shoulder

26 The ridge

27 The spur

28 The neck

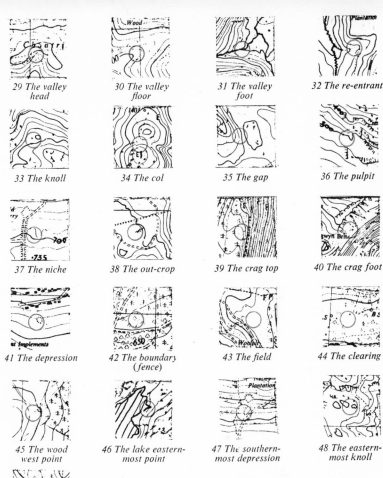

29 The valley head

30 The valley floor

31 The valley foot

32 The re-entrant

33 The knoll

34 The col

35 The gap

36 The pulpit

37 The niche

38 The out-crop

39 The crag top

40 The crag foot

41 The depression

42 The boundary (fence)

43 The field

44 The clearing

45 The wood west point

46 The lake easternmost point

47 The southernmost depression

48 The easternmost knoll

49 The trig. point

MAP 3

Control Terminology and Definition of Features

1. Controls shall be marked on Master Maps by RED circles of ½ cm. in diameter. The situation of the control shall be in the exact middle of this circle – but NOT indicated by a 'dot'.

2. When the control feature exists on the map as well as on the ground then the brief verbal description of the site shall include the 'definite article', e.g. *The* track-end, or *The* foot-bridge.

3. When the control feature exists on the ground but is not shown on the map, then the description shall include the 'Indefinite article' e.g. *A* stile on the track, or *A* tall pine.

4. A six-figure map reference shall be included in the designation of the control.

5. Controls shall be numbered on the Master-Maps.

6. For cross-country events the Controls shall be joined together by a red line on the Master-Map, indicating the shape of the course.

MAP 4

REFERENCE

Yds 1,000   500   0   1,000 Yds

Roads

Ministry of Transport

Motorway & Class I Dual Carriageway	M 4 A 123
Class I	A123
„ 2	Fenced B 2314 Unfenced
„ Under Construction	
Other Roads	Good, metalled Poor, or unmetalled
Footpaths	FP FP
	Fenced Unfenced

Railways, Multiple Track ... Station   Road over   FB
Sidings   Cutting   Tunnel   (Footbridge)

„ Single Track   Viaduct   Level Crossing   Embankment   Road under

„ Narrow Gauge

LTE & Glasgow District Subway Stations ... O   Interchange Stations ... ⊗

Aerial Ropeway   Aerial Ropeway

Boundaries { County or County Borough
       „ „ County of City (in Scotland)
       „ „ „ „ „ „ with Parish
       „ Parish

Pipe Line (Oil, Water)   Pipe Line

Electricity Transmission Lines (Pylons shown at bends and spaced conventionally) — ⊕ – – – – ⊕

Post Offices (In Villages & Rural Areas only) ... P   Town Hall ... TH   Public House ... PH

Church or Chapel with Tower ▮ Church or Chapel with Spire ▯ Church or Chapel without either ✛

Triangulation Station ... △   on Church with Tower ... ⧄   without Tower ... ⧄

Intersected Point on Chy. O   on Church with Spire ... ◊   without Spire ... +   on Building ... ▬

Guide Post GP.   Mile Post MP.   Mile Stone MS.   Boundary Stone BS •   Boundary Post BP•

Youth Hostel Y   Telephone Call Box (Public) T   (AA) A   (RAC) R   Antiquity (site of) ✛

Public Buildings ▬	Glasshouses □▫
Quarry & Gravel Pit	Orchard
National Trust Area (Sheen Common NT)	Furze
„ „ „ Scotland ... NTS	Rough Pasture Heath & Moor
Osier Bed	Marsh
Reeds	Well ... u ○
Park, Fenced	Spring ... Spr ○
	Wind Pump ... Wd Pp.
Wood, Coniferous, Fenced	
Wood, Non-Coniferous Unfenced	Contours are at 25 feet vertical interval, shown broken in built up areas.
Brushwood, Fenced & Unfenced	Spot Height ... 123 •

Ferries   Sand Hills
Foot   Vehicle   Mud   Flat Rock

LUMMI   Slopes   △ Beacon

Lake   Sand   Lightship
Bridge   Lock   Highest point to which Medium Tides flow   Sand
Towing   Aqueduct   Weir   & Shingle
Path   Ford   FB   Cliff
Dam   (Footbridge)   Lighthouse ▮

Place on object

ROMER
Cut along outer edges of Scale

500m

Map symbols for the 2½″ to the mile scale map.

Särtryck ur Stern-bladet

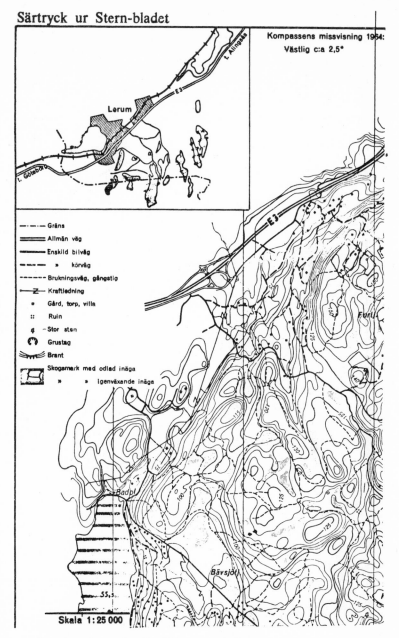

Lerum

Gräns

Allmän väg

Enskild bilväg

» körväg

Brukningsväg, gångstig

Kraftledning

Gård, torp, villa

Ruin

Stor sten

Grustag

Brant

Skogsmark med odlad inäga

» » igenväxande inäga

Badpl

Bävsjön

Skala 1:25 000

A section of a modern Swedish map, which has been especially prepared for orienteering. The original is in four colours – blue, green, brown and black.

MAP 5

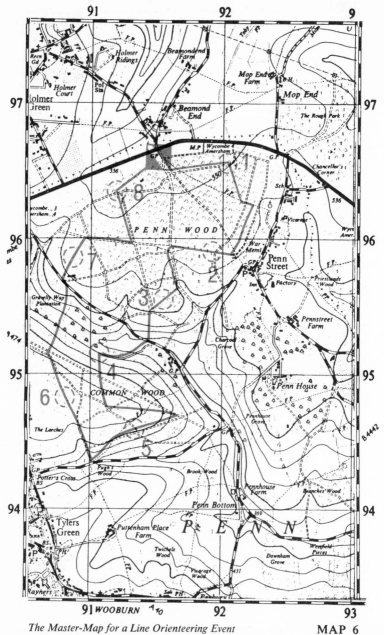

The Master-Map for a Line Orienteering Event   **MAP 6**

Note: The secret controls, shown here by dotted circles, are not included
on the Master-Map.

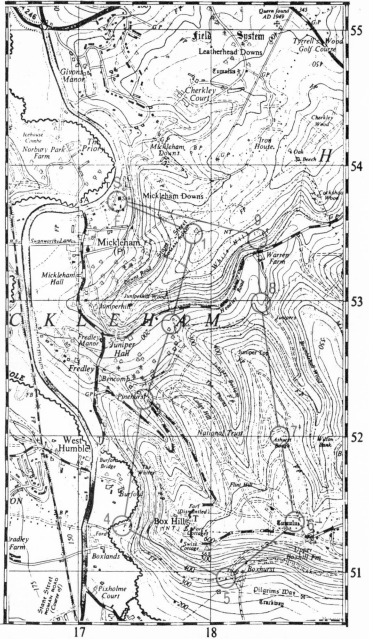

The Master-Map for the Novices' Event. The nine-control route traverses through the woods around Box Hill, Surrey. The description of the controls is given on page 34.

MAP 7

MAP 8

The Map Symbols for the new 2nd Series $2\frac{1}{2}''$ to the mile Ordnance Survey Map. Footpaths that are also rights of way are marked by green dashed lines. Other improvements include the representation of trees and rocks by new and more comprehensive signs.

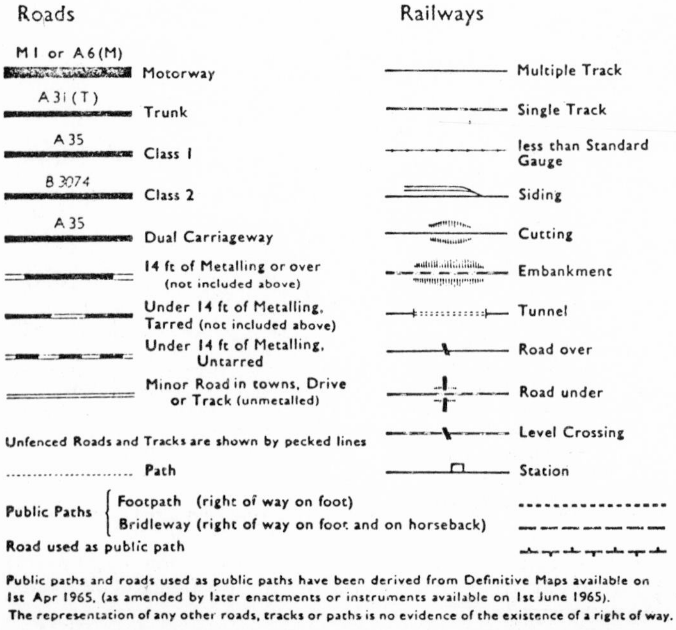

Roads

M 1 or A 6 (M) ▬▬▬▬▬ Motorway

A 3i (T) ▬▬▬▬▬ Trunk

A 35 ▬▬▬▬▬ Class 1

B 3074 ▬▬▬▬▬ Class 2

A 35 ▬▬▬▬▬ Dual Carriageway

═══════ 14 ft of Metalling or over (not included above)

▬▬▬▬ Under 14 ft of Metalling, Tarred (not included above)

▬ ▬ ▬ Under 14 ft of Metalling, Untarred

═══════ Minor Road in towns, Drive or Track (unmetalled)

Unfenced Roads and Tracks are shown by pecked lines

.... Path

Public Paths { Footpath (right of way on foot)
Bridleway (right of way on foot and on horseback)

Road used as public path

Railways

───────── Multiple Track

─ ─ ─ ─ ─ Single Track

· — · — · — less than Standard Gauge

═══════ Siding

───────── Cutting

───────── Embankment

—┼··········┼— Tunnel

───────── Road over

───────── Road under

─ ─ ─ ─ ─ Level Crossing

───□─── Station

· · · · · · · · · ·

▬ ▬ ▬ ▬ ▬

▬┷▬┷▬┷▬┷▬

Public paths and roads used as public paths have been derived from Definitive Maps available on 1st Apr 1965, (as amended by later enactments or instruments available on 1st June 1965). The representation of any other roads, tracks or paths is no evidence of the existence of a right of way.

MAP 9

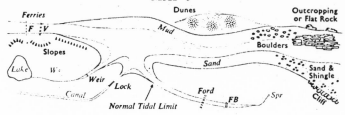

Rock Features

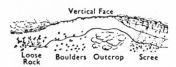

Loose Rock   Boulders   Outcrop   Scree

Heights

Heights are in feet above Mean Sea Level at Newlyn.

165 .	Determined by ground survey
913 .	Determined by air survey
250 200 150 125	Contours are at 25 feet vertical interval.

Abbreviations

BP		Boundary Post
BS		Boundary Stone
CH		Club House
F		Ferries, Foot
V		Ferries, Vehicular
FB		Footbridge
Ho		House
MP		Mile Post
MS		Mile Stone
Mon		Monument
P		Post Office
Pol Sta	Rural Areas only	Police Station
PC		Public Convenience
PH		Public House
Sch		School
Spr		Spring
T		Telephone, Public
A		Telephone, AA
R		Telephone, RAC
TH		Town Hall
Twr		Tower
W		Well
Wd Pp		Wind Pump
Y		Youth Hostel

Vegetation

	Trees, Coniferous
	Trees, Non Coniferous
	Trees, Mixed
	Coppice
	Orchard
	Scrub
	Bracken
	Heath
	Rough Grassland
	Reeds
	Marsh
	Saltings

Compilation Notes

NC 46 NW 1961	NC 46 NE 1961	NC 56 NW 1962	NC 56 NE 1962
NC 46 SW 1961	NC 46 SE 1961	NC 56 SW 1961	NC 56 SE 1962

The sheet numbers and dates shown are those of the component Six Inch sheets from which this map is compiled.

Major roads revised 1964.

MAP 10

Boundaries   Revised to 1-6-64.

— — — — —	Geographical County
— — — — — — —	Administrative County, County Borough, or County of City
- - - - - - - - - - -	Municipal Borough, Urban District, Rural District, Burgh or District Council
· · · · · · · · · · · · · ·	Civil Parish
— — — — — — —	Borough Constituency, Burgh Constituency or County Constituency

The first appropriate symbol in this list is shown when coincidence of boundaries occurs

Shown alternately with one of the symbols above, when coincidence of boundaries occurs

Shown only when not coincident with other boundaries

Symbols

	Church or Chapel		
♦	Church or Chapel	with Tower	
♦	,,	with Spire	
+	,,	without Tower or Spire	
▭		Roofed Building	
▨		Glasshouse	
▱		Ruin	
○		Chimney	
➤		Bus & Coach Station	
⚏		Lighthouse	
⚓		Lightship	
△		Triangulation Station	
♦ ♦ ÷ ⚏		Triangulation Point on Church, Chapel or Lighthouse	
▱ ○		Triangulation Point on Building - Chimney	
- - - - - - - - -		Telephone Lines	

┌ N T S ┐	National Trust always open
┌ NTS ┐	National Trust opening restricted
VILLA	Roman Antiquities (AD 43 to AD 420)
Castle	Other Antiquities
✛	Site of Antiquity
✕ 1066	Site of Battle
◗	Gravel Pit
◗	Sand Pit
◗	Other Pits
◗	Quarry
⬭	Refuse & Slag Heaps
▨▨▨▨	Sloping Masonry

Electricity Transmission Lines

- - -●- - -	- - - - - - - -
with Pylons	with Posts

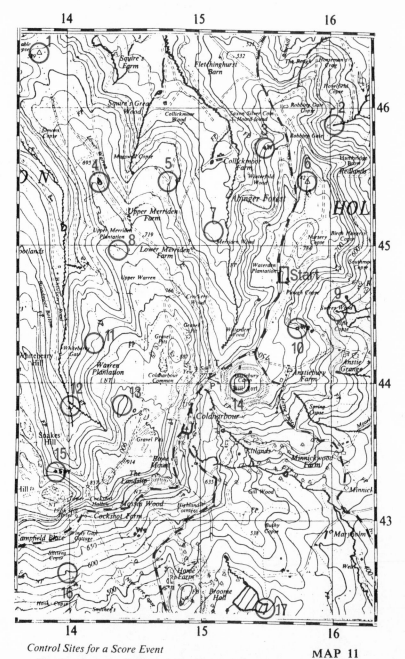

Control Sites for a Score Event

MAP 11

The description and points value of the seventeen controls is given on page 140.

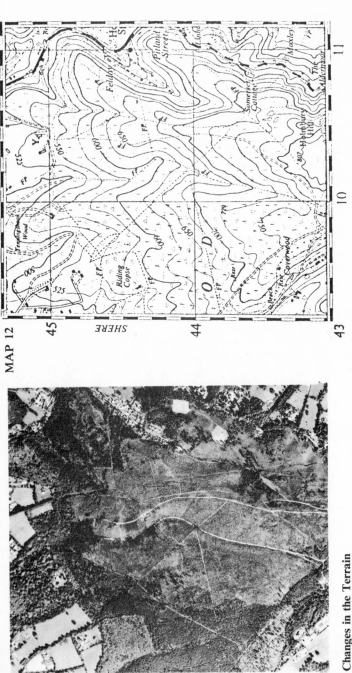

MAP 12

Changes in the Terrain

The aerial photograph of the same area covered by the map shows several differences, even although the map is only four years old.

The photograph picks out many more paths on the heath and indicates many short-cuts between paths shown on the map. It also shows a new very prominent path running from the 'reservoir' (094437) north-east to the fields and houses. This path, not marked on the map, is actually the line of a new water-pipe ditch which has produced a track since the map was drawn.

The photograph also shows that the even-forest shown by the map all across the 44 Northing, has been drastically cut

ORIENTEERING

With some practice the interpretation of the contours becomes second nature for the orienteer. He soon recognizes at a glance what each formation of lines portrays; valleys, cliffs, ridges, concave and convex slopes have legible signatures written clearly for all to learn how to read.

The more common features are shown in Maps 2 and 3.

F. *Magnetic Variation*

This aspect of compass work is explained in the chapter dealing with the Compass and Bearings. It will be seen that it is important that certain information is included on this aspect of way-finding at the edge of all orienteering maps.

G. *A Code of Ethics*

The prosperous expansion of orienteering depends to a large extent on the good-will of the various landowners in this country. At all times it is necessary to preserve and foster that good-will and trust.

Contrary to general opinion, there is no such thing in this country as unowned land. Even the rugged flanks of the mountains and the sweep of desolate moorlands are someone's property. Luckily the ownership of many areas which are suitable for orienteering is vested in the State or the Crown, but even then there are certain by-laws and rules which must be observed and kept. Common Land, National Trust Property and the Royal Parks, together with Forestry Commission Land, all offer delightful terrain for map and compass work, but all of them need permission before use.

The Ordnance Survey maps conscientiously point out that the representation on the map of a path or track does not infer that there is a right of way. Unless the magic letters—F.P.—are marked on the path you are not entitled to be there by law.

The race organizer will, of course, negotiate with the various 'land-owners' for permission to use the area for a race. He will also mark-off any area included on his map that is strictly private.

The adoption of a courteous attitude towards people's gardens, planted fields, plantations of young trees and crops in general is not just an arbitrary affair for the competitor. The Rules of Orienteering (*see* Chapter 10) make it very clear that anti-social conduct will result in disqualification and that the orienteer himself is responsible for any damage or trespassing that he does.

Our sport depends upon the co-operation of the land-user—whether he be an allotment holder or a Forestry Commission District Officer, in the area we wish to use. It is vital that we observe the Country Code at all times.

H. *Ordnance Survey Copyright*

Every authorized reproduction of areas of an Ordnance Survey Map must make an acknowledgement.

Permission to reproduce O.S. work can be obtained from the Director General of Ordnance Survey and there is a set scale of royalties that are payable.

The regulations governing reproduction of maps and the procedure necessary to become licensed to do so are explained in Chapter 8.

'. . . *the map needs protecting from rain and sweat.*'

The Compass

A piece of magnetized ore-bearing rock suspended from a thong or a vine was probably the first form of compass to be used. It is difficult to discover who first realized that such a piece of rock always pointed in the same direction, but the Chinese seem to have understood its secrets at least 4,000 years ago. It was that great 'orienteer' Marco Polo—one of his over-land courses went from Italy to China—who brought back the knowledge of the compass from Cathay in 1260. Until this time Europeans had had to manage with the sun and the north star for navigation.

Today's modern orienteering compass is a deal more convenient to use and carry than a piece of rock, and yet it is basically just as simple in principle. A small magnetized needle suspended in a housing always swings to point towards north.

The orienteer has a choice of several suitable compasses and nearly all the desirable models are made by the same company —SILVA. This Swedish firm is directed by three brothers— Bjorn, Alvar and Arvid Kjellström, all of whom were enthusiastic orienteers in the 1930's and invented a compass combined with a protractor to help them win races. This family business still gives tremendous support to the sport of orienteering and through its business interests is responsible for the spread of the game throughout the world.

An orienteer is absorbed at least half the time with the problem of finding a bearing or, in other words, locating a direction, from the map. For this operation he does not need the services of a magnetic needle, but rather the use of a protractor. The 'Silva' compass is also a device for measuring angles or finding a bearing, so that this instrument fulfils the two needs of the orienteer. It can find the correct direction from the map and it can point it out on the ground.

The cheapest protractor-type compass, best recommended for school use or for the novice who is poor, is the Type 5 'Silva' model, which costs 15s. 6d. It is a well made instrument that will satisfy your needs until such a time as you become more ambitious and split-seconds suddenly matter.

The more expensive models produced by 'Silva' are the Type 3 at 28s. 6d, and the Type 4 at 39s. 6d. Although these two compasses work on exactly the same principles as the cheaper model they do have two refinements which make them quicker to use. Firstly, their needles are suspended in a liquid-filled housing, which means that the needle settles down quickly to point in the right direction. On the Type 5 the needle is brought to rest by induction dampening. Secondly, the needle housings have transparent bases on the dearer models, and this means that it is much easier to be accurate when using the compass as a protractor. (Figure 23).

The only merit of the Type 4 over the Type 3, is that it is bigger and more robust. With its 5-in. long base plate and large needle housing it makes accuracy possible at speed.

Bearings

A bearing is a horizontal angle fixing a point in respect to North. It is measured in a clockwise direction from North in degrees. There are 360° in a full circle. (In Sweden a metric right angle has been adopted which produces 400° in a circle.)

In Figure 5, B is on a bearing of 120° and C on a bearing of 240° from the point A.

An early complication to the learning process is the existence of three Norths (Fig. 6).

TRUE NORTH is the actual direction of the North Pole and can be ignored for all practical purposes by the orienteer.

GRID NORTH is the direction in which all the vertical grid lines—the Eastings—point on an Ordnance Survey map.

MAGNETIC NORTH is the direction towards which the magnetic needle points, i.e. the magnetic pole.

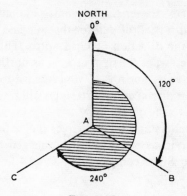

FIGURE 5

Bearings

'B' is on a bearing of 120° and 'C' is on a bearing of 240° from the point 'A'.

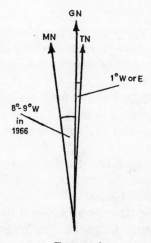

FIGURE 6

The Three Norths

The orienteer is only interested in the variation between Grid North and Magnetic North. The location of True North is only of academic interest.

ORIENTEERING

Like the feast of Easter the magnetic pole moves from year to year and its direction of pull for the compass needle seldom coincides with the direction of Grid north. This difference in direction between what the map accepts as north and what the compass points to as north is of vital interest to the orienteer. All through your orienteering career you will be converting one kind of bearing to the other.

In order to understand the principles that a protractor-compass works on, it is necessary to learn some general terms, rules and parts of the 'Silva' compass. (*See* Plate 4.)

Compass Work 1—Which Direction?

All compass work in orienteering is divided into two sections; the first is concerned with finding the right direction on the ground from the information given on the map. To do this it is necessary to take a bearing first from the map.

To take a Grid bearing

1. Place the long edge of the compass along the desired line of travel, i.e. join up where you are to where you wish to reach. Check that the Direction of Travel arrow points towards your destination.

2. Turn the compass housing until the orienting lines and arrow are parallel to the grid lines.

3. Read off the number of degrees at the index pointer. This is the Grid Bearing.

It is essential to appreciate that this bearing is of academic interest only—it must be converted to a Magnetic bearing before it is of practical interest.

In this country the discrepancy between the Grid and Magnetic North is too large to ignore. This 'magnetic variation' is quoted at the foot of every Ordnance Survey map, it is also shown in diagrammatic form. The variation not only differs from place to place in Britain but it is also changing slightly from year to year. The annual change is also indicated at the foot of the map.

The organizer of an orienteering race will either provide the

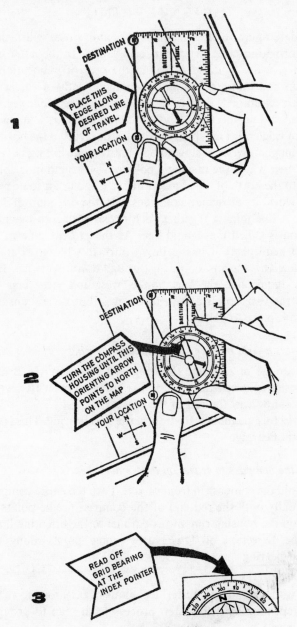

1 PLACE THIS EDGE ALONG DESIRED LINE OF TRAVEL

DESTINATION

YOUR LOCATION

2 TURN THE COMPASS HOUSING UNTIL THIS ORIENTING ARROW POINTS TO NORTH ON THE MAP

DESTINATION

YOUR LOCATION

3 READ OFF GRID BEARING AT THE INDEX POINTER

FIGURE 7
Taking a grid bearing

up-to-date figure for the magnetic variation or he will include the information necessary for its calculation. In the latter case he will give the figure as it was in the year of publication of the map and indicate the annual change. At the moment the magnetic variation is decreasing by about $\frac{1}{2}°$ every four years in Scotland and northern England and about every six years in the south of England. This change is due to the fact that the position of the magnetic pole is slowly, but constantly, shifting.

The area which the magnetic pole moves around in is somewhere to the north of the Hudson Bay in Canada. In some parts of the world its attraction coincides with the direction of True North. A line joining together such places with zero magnetic variation is called the agonic line. At the present time in the western hemisphere it passes down through Chicago south to near New Orleans and on down through South America. East of this agonic line the variation is west and vice versa. In Britain the variation is always to the west but varies considerably from place to place.

To convert a Grid bearing to a Magnetic bearing

1. Read off or calculate the Magnetic variation. (In Britain and Western Europe the variation is going to be West several degrees for at least the rest of the century.)

2. Add this magnetic variation to the grid bearing. This is the Magnetic Bearing.

To use the compass to travel on a Magnetic bearing

1. Hold the compass in front of you. Turn the entire compass horizontally until the red end of the compass needle points to North on the housing rim and is parallel to the orienting lines.

2. The Direction of Travel arrow now points along the required bearing.

This is the 'bread and butter' technique of orienteering and is worth repeating as a four-step process from map to ground. (*See* Figure 8.)

ORIENTEERING

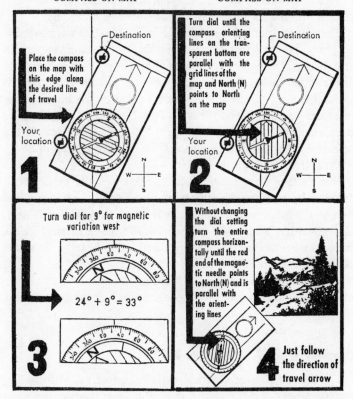

COMPASS ON MAP   COMPASS ON MAP

Place the compass on the map with this edge along the desired line of travel

Destination

Your location

1

N
W — E
S

Turn dial until the compass orienting lines on the transparent bottom are parallel with the grid lines of the map and North (N) points to North on the map

Destination

Your location

2

N
W — E
S

Turn dial for 9° for magnetic variation west

24° + 9° = 33°

3

Without changing the dial setting turn the entire compass horizontally until the red end of the magnetic needle points to North (N) and is parallel with the orienting lines

Just follow the direction of travel arrow

4

COMPASS REMOVED FROM MAP   COMPASS REMOVED FROM MAP

FIGURE 8

The Four-Step Technique for finding a bearing on the map, converting it to a magnetic bearing and sighting with it in the field.

1. Place the long edge of the compass along the desired line of travel.

2. Turn the compass housing until the orienting arrow is parallel to the grid lines and points to the top of the map.

3. Add the magnetic variation by twisting the housing anti-clockwise 9° (or whatever the M.V. is).

4. Hold the compass in front of you and turn round until the red end of the compass needle points to North on the housing-rim.

ORIENTEERING

This process is as simple as saying one, two, three, four—and should become as natural to the orienteer as counting.

The clever orienteer can 'sight' his compass with remarkable accuracy. He does this by making sure that the compass is held exactly at right angles to the place of his chest—that it sticks out like another nose. Rather than twisting just the compass to allow the needle to point to the north point on the housing, the orienteer turns his whole body. This method of aligning the compass needle means that when the compass is set all the orienteer does is to lift his eyes and he is looking straight along the required bearing.

One further elementary precaution enables the experienced racer to get a correct reading every time from his compass; it is that he remembers that the needle is affected by iron and steel. Consequently, he doesn't carry a whistle made of steel in his breast pocket or lean on an iron gate to take a bearing. Even the clip on a ball-point pen will swing a compass needle some 10 degrees if it is held next to the housing. Attention to detail can make all the difference to being lost or finding the control first try.

Compass Work 2—Where am I?

The second part of compass work is concerned with finding out just where you are on the map. For this operation the compass is first used to find a Magnetic bearing.

To take a Magnetic bearing

1. Hold the compass horizontally so that the direction-of-travel arrow points at the selected feature.

2. Keep the base of the compass in this position and twist the housing until North on the housing rim is opposite the red end of the compass needle.

3. Read off the number of degrees at the index pointer. This is the Magnetic bearing.

Just as a Grid bearing is useless for work in the field until it has been converted, so is this Magnetic bearing valueless on the map until it has been changed to a Grid figure.

ORIENTEERING

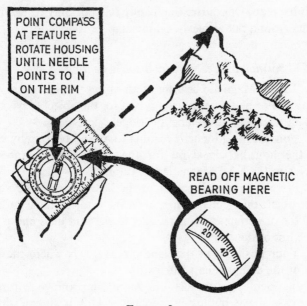

FIGURE 9
Taking a magnetic bearing

To convert a Magnetic bearing to a Grid bearing

1. Read off or calculate the Magnetic variation—it will be about 9° west in the U.K.

2. Subtract this variation from the Magnetic bearing. This is the Grid bearing.

The mnemonic—'*M*anchester *G*rammar *S*chool', *m*agnetic to grid *s*ubtract, has been a great help to me on many occasions.

By taking Magnetic bearings of various identifiable objects it is possible to use this information to locate your position on the map—and hence find out exactly where you are. This skill is often used by the orienteer to check his position, if not to find it completely. Often the puzzled orienteer is only half lost. He knows, for instance, that he is on a certain lane or astride a particular ridge but does not know exactly how far along the feature he is positioned. He can pin-point his position on the map by taking a Magnetic bearing of a nearby feature and projecting it on his map. Of course, the feature has not only to be visible on the ground but also exist on the map.

To find position on a feature by a single bearing

1. Take a Magnetic bearing of an object to one side of your position. For better accuracy it is best for the object to be nearly at right angles to your 'lane' or 'ridge'.

2. Convert this Magnetic reading to a Grid bearing by twisting the housing clockwise for the appropriate number of degrees in the local Magnetic variation.

3. Place a 'long-end' corner of the base plate on the identifiable object on the map. Then pivot the whole compass around until the orienting arrow is parallel to the grid lines and points to the top of the map.

4. Your position on the 'lane' or 'ridge' is where the long edge of the compass cuts the feature.

If the orienteer is not just 'misplaced' on a known feature, as in the case above, but lost in more general terms, he can still use the compass to locate his position. ᵀn this case he needs to be able to carry out the above procedure with two recognizable objects.

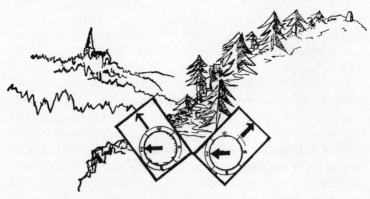

FIGURE 10
1. Take a bearing of the feature.
2. Convert this magnetic bearing to a grid bearing, e.g. subtract 9°.

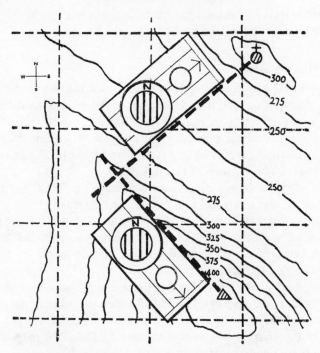

3. Place the long-side front corner of the base-plate on the identifiable object on the map. Then pivot the whole compass around until the orienting arrow is parallel to the grid lines and points to the north on the map. Draw a line along the edge of the compass. Repeat for second identifiable object. Position is where the two lines cross.

To find position by taking bearings on two features

Steps 1–3 as directed above and in Figure 10.

4. Draw a faint line of the map along the long edge of the compass.

5. Repeat for the second feature.

6. Where the two lines cross is your position.

More accuracy could be obtained by taking three bearings and projecting three lines on the map. Then your position would be somewhere in the triangle made by their junction. In practice it is often difficult to find two suitable recognizable features, never mind three, and in any case the ground features themselves should start to fall into place with the map once the search for position has been narrowed to a hundred-metre square.

Setting the Map

Without any question it is the map that is the most basic tool in orienteering and the successful orienteer will solve most problems of route-finding without resorting to further aid than is found within its margins. The compass, important as it is, should only be regarded as a 'secondary' line of defence, to be fallen back on in times of real difficulty.

The expert orienteer, as he runs through the forest, contours round a ridge or crosses a valley, will be continually 'setting' his map in his hands so that the panorama of the countryside coincides with the lay-out of the map. A map is called 'set' when directions on it correspond to the directions of the same features on the ground.

If, for instance, he is travelling north along a path, then he will be holding the map and looking at it with the printing the right way up, but should he turn to run southwards he will at once twist the map around so that the north edge of the map is towards him and the printing upside down.

The relative position of the printing matters hardly at all to the good orienteer. In any case, names seldom offer a contribution to his way-finding knowledge. It is the contours and the symbols depicting the various features that are important, and these look 'right' from whichever direction they are viewed.

With the map set in the hands everything slots into place. If the map indicates that there is a church with a spire on a hill to the right, then a quick glance to the right proves the point; if it shows that there will be a small lake on the left after half a mile, then sure enough the water will be seen on the left after several minutes' travel.

In the event of the orienteer wishing to set his map on a featureless common, or in a thick wood, or at night, where no obvious features are easily visible for the purposes of alignment, the map can be set accurately with the compass.

ORIENTEERING

Setting the Map with a Compass (Figure 11)

1. Twist the compass housing round until the appropriate Magnetic variation figure is opposite the index pointer.

2. With the map on a flat surface, place the compass so that the direction-of-travel arrow is over a vertical grid line and pointing to the top edge of the map.

3. Turn the map around, with the compass on it, until the red end of the compass needle points to North on the rim of the compass housing.

The map is now set.

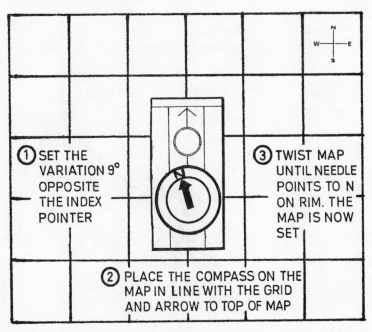

FIGURE 11

Setting the map by using a compass

Back bearings

The orienteer often feels insecure as he struggles across difficult country and needs to check that he is still travelling in the right direction—or on the correct bearing. This situation can

63

easily happen when climbing a wooded hillside. Suppose that after leaving a stream junction and climbing on a bearing—a forward bearing—across a 'featureless' hillside, (too many similar trees can be just as negative as no features at all) the orienteer fears that he has strayed from his course. Perhaps several fallen trees had prevented a direct path being always taken and now he wishes to re-establish his position. Like Lot's wife, to check his position all he needs to do is turn round. Without altering his compass setting he sights back on to the stream junction in the valley. If he is still on the right course the white end of the compass needle will be pointing to North on the housing rim.

This technique is making use of a 'back-bearing' and as you will see from Figure 12 there is no need to make any change to

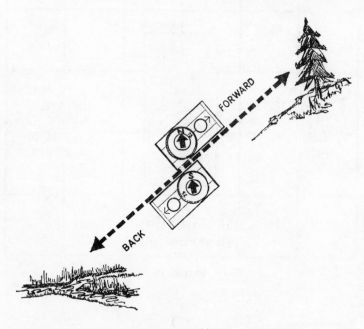

FIGURE 12

Forward and Back Bearings

The compass reading is left the same; only the needle is pointed 180° round to obtain the back bearing, i.e. to 'S' rather than 'N'.

ORIENTEERING

the compass setting. The change is produced in direction by taking note of the different ends of the compass needle—the red end for a forward bearing, the white for a back.

Many books on map-reading explain back bearings with reference to adding on and taking off 180°; in practical orienteering such a process wastes precious seconds, and, more important, is a glorious opportunity for inaccuracy as well. Anyone who has attempted at speed, with sweat in the eyes, to subtract

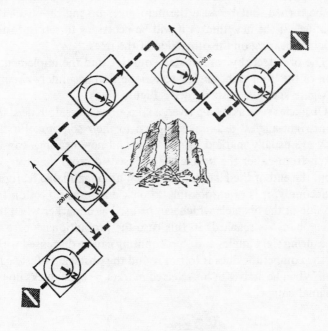

FIGURE 13

The Four-Right-Angles Technique
The obstacle can be avoided and the original bearing returned to after the cliff has been bypassed. The first and third changes in direction should be equal in distance. NOTE: The bearing is not altered at each corner; only the needle is aligned on a different point of the compass.

180° from a bearing like 317° and then spin the housing to set this new figure, will recognize at least two potential sources of error!

Circumnavigating an Obstacle

It sometimes happens that forward progress on a bearing is prevented by an impassable obstacle which isn't expected because it is not marked on the map. A thick forestry plantation often produces this kind of barrier. Obviously, the obstacle has to be turned, but because the map gives no indication of the confines of the new thicket it will be necessary to return to the original bearing on the other side of the trees.

The orienteer, by careful step-counting and the implementation of the 'four right angles' technique, can accurately circumnavigate such an obstacle. (*See* Figure 13.)

Obstacles such as a deep river, a lake, or a cliff seldom need the 'four-right-angles' technique applied to their solution. Firstly, they are usually marked on the map and new bearings can be taken from either the bridge that is used to cross the river, or from the end of the lake or cliff, which are identifiable features.

Secondly, it is often possible to pick out some object on the far side of the obstacle which can be used as a marker when the other 'bank' is reached. In this case the precautionary care of measuring right angles and step-counting can be dispensed with; all the competitor does is to run round the obstacle as fast as he can. When he arrives at his selected marker he again picks up his original course.

'. . . the compass needle always points to North.'

5

Decision Making

The course-setter for an orienteering race is constantly seeking to involve the competitor in schismatic situations. His aim in life is to present several alternative routes between Controls, and to do it so cleverly that the orienteer has to think carefully before selecting a particular course of action. From the competitors' point of view nothing sets the 'adrenalin' secreting into the blood-stream faster than the prospect of a difficult decision to be made. The situation where the legs are all set to start off running down the nearest obvious path, while the mind is engaged in the prospect of a direct route through the trees, is one that rapidly produces a feeling of insecurity. All orienteers have experienced this conflict of emotions and know that it can produce a partial paralysis of the body and a clouding over of the brain.

It is when he is in this 'stale-mate' attitude that the orienteer makes some of his most colossal blunders. I remember watching a senior competitor, who should have known better, sway from foot to foot in front of a thickly planted and overgrown wood. A detour to the left or to the right would have avoided the obstacle with ease, but his powers of reasoning were temporarily suspended. With the presentation of such an equal choice of evasive action he could only compromise and he headed straight into the 'jungle' where he was heard but not seen for the next twenty minutes.

It is therefore necessary for the orienteer to have certain basic principles to follow when he is required to make a decision about choice of routes. His decision should be a rational one made in the light of all the available evidence.

ORIENTEERING

Basically, his choice of routes is governed by one paramount question, which he must ask himself: 'As a straight line is the shortest distance between two points—why can't I take it?'

His answer to this leading question is based on the following factors:

1. Because there are physical obstacles in the way such as:
(a) a high hill, or a deep valley;
(b) a wide river, lake or cliff;
(c) private property, or cultivated farm land;
(d) thick overgrown forest or marsh land.

2. Because there is a nearby path which links the controls together.

3. Because, the control point being where it is, it will be best to be 'caught' by some obvious feature to its left or right.

4. Because of my personal talents and preferences another way is more acceptable.

The rapid sifting of evidence and the weighing-up of the pros and cons of alternative plans is what the sport of orienteering is all about. Each way of going from one control to another will have certain advantages as well as compensations. The experienced orienteer develops a sensitive calculating mechanism which computes distance against height to be climbed; path running against forest scrambling; and ease of route-finding against complex navigation. Finally, when the variables have been 'costed-out' on a time basis, the whole equation needs to be considered in the light of his own fitness. Obviously, the decision to tackle a physically hard section might be questioned early on in a race, when even pace judgement is a high priority, but the same section might well be justified as a choice of route near the end of a race by a still strong runner.

As was said earlier on in this chapter, 'all decisions should be rational ones', and so it is best to study and learn several rules of thumb that can be applied to stock situations.

The long easy way v. the short tough route

This is the most common choice which the orienteer meets in a competition. Will the well-trodden path around the area be quicker than a direct crossing? The answer will depend on what the surface of the direct route presents to the hurrying orienteer. The good runner will be able to cover about a mile in less than eight minutes on a flat path, the average performer may well take about ten minutes; but what they both need to know is their possible speed in rougher terrain.

It is well worthwhile compiling some figures for your own average speed on different types of surface, so that a valid comparison can be made between the advantages of one route over another.

(a) For a beaten-down path surface

(b) For a heather, bracken and heath land surface

(c) For a mature forest with occasional fallen trees and low branches.

(d) For a thick forest with undergrowth and occasional brambles, etc.

In respect of the last type of 'going', there is, of course, the even more inhospitable area of thick hawthorn where progress is measured by the hour rather than the minute.

Experiments I carried out for my own information give the following average times for a 400-metre stretch of the above 'going' on flattish terrain.

(a) The path ..	..	2 minutes.
(b) Heath land..	..	3 minutes.
(c) Open forest	..	6 minutes.
(d) Thick forest	..	10 minutes.

These figures make far more sense and acquire a more practical look if they are converted to ratios, e.g. $5 \times a = d$, or $2 \times b = c$. In other words, a path round a thick forest can be five times longer and still be as quick; or 1,000 metres of heath can be covered in the same time as 500 metres of open forest.

The diagram on page 70 will give you a visual impression of these ratios—but remember these are my average figures. Your own set of ratios will be much more valuable and can be obtained by half an hour's exercise in a nearby forest.

You will have noticed that the use of metres rather than yards as a unit of distance is prevalent in orienteering. There is nothing *avant-garde* about this attitude. The orienteer is not anticipating the coming of the metric system, but just making use of the most

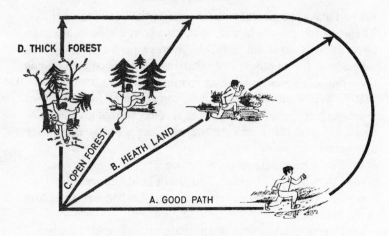

FIGURE 14

The long easy way v. *the short tough route*

convenient unit of measure printed on the 1 : 25,000 map. The grid lines are excellent guides for estimating 1,000 metres (about 1,093 yards), and the black and white 'diced' border gives a quick indication of the size of a 100-metres section (about 109 yards).

Many orienteers adapt the front edge of their compass to make a '100-metre rule'. They cut out a section of the 'dicing' from the border of a map and stick it to the edge of the base-plate (*see* Figure 15).

FIGURE 15

100-metre scale for 2½" map

Height ascended v. a detour around

No physical exercise can expend energy so rapidly as climbing up-hill. Athletes running on a horizontal tread-mill can carry on for hours, but should the physiologist in charge of the experiment wish to exhaust the runner quickly he just tilts the machine 15°, and within minutes the athlete is finished.

To raise the body weighing 150 lb. up 100 ft. vertically is a substantial amount of work. Consequently, the orienteer should look twice at any route which crosses 'unproductive' contours. By 'unproductive' contours we mean height that is not retained during the traverse from control to control. Obviously, where the next control is 300 ft. above the position of its predecessor there can be no evading at least 300 ft. of ascent. However, the clever course-setter often places a steep hill or a deep valley in between two controls of similar altitude, and the orienteer has to decide if a 'contouring' route around the obstacle is worth while.

Again it is the comparative speed that is important and with some personal experiment it is possible to equate height in terms of distance, so that two alternative routes can be compared.

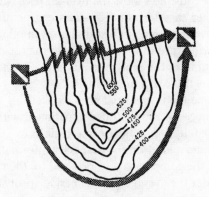

FIGURE 16

Height v. *Distance*

The northern direct route over the hill is 1 kilometres long and involves a climb of 200 feet. Using the formula of 25 ft. = 100 metres, this produces a figure of 800 metres, to give a total of 1,800 metres. This figure still compares favourably with the southern route around the hill which measures two kilometres. Therefore the best choice for the fit orienteer is to go over the hill.

ORIENTEERING

Personally I find that on sections longer than a kilometre a 25-ft. contour rise is equivalent to 100 metres on the flat. For example, I know that I can cross one grid square faster on the flat than I can cover half that distance and ascend 125 ft. In fact, the flat route is about one minute faster.

My formula for this situation is: 'For the detour to be profitable it must be less than the direct distance plus 100 metres for every 25 ft. climbed.' (*See* Figure 16.)

This equation assumes that the type of surface encountered is the same in each case, but often the detour can make use of good paths, and this must seriously tip the scales against the 'up and over' route, for nothing is more frustrating and tiring than vertical jungle!

The Use of Guide Line Features

If the average speed for a race is calculated it always comes as a surprise to see just how slow the over-all pace can be, even in a race held over easy terrain. Top-class cross-country runners are used to covering a mile in just under seven minutes, and yet in an orienteering race of the same length they seldom manage to break ten minutes for each mile and are often nearer twelve. Where then has this extra time gone?

Far more time than is realized goes on checking the map and using the compass. A simple timed experiment with a map will soon show that it is practically impossible to stop running, orientate the map and glean the necessary information in under 15 seconds. If the compass is also resorted to, then a time of 30 seconds is nearer the average for this period spent standing still. In difficult country the orienteer is likely to affirm his position from the map ten times a mile—and that delay alone will account for at least three minutes of 'wasted' time in ten.

It is obvious that the fewer times the map is consulted the better. Some orienteers have developed fabulous photographic memories. Magne Lysfad, a Norwegian forestry worker, is able to memorize ten square inches of a map at a glance and then run confidently through the terrain ticking-off in his head paths, valleys and streams as he reaches them. This facility helped him become the winner of the first European Championships in 1962.

ORIENTEERING

Even without such a gift for remembering detail, the orienteer can reduce the number of stoppages for map consultation by making use of 'guide-line' features. By using easily identifiable features as mental 'hand-rails' he can be guided positively and at speed for many sections of a course. Obviously, a path or track is the best guide-line possible, but in pathless country there are still many other equally reliable features that can be used. Ridges, valleys, and streams can be used as constant checks for direction. Man-made items, such as fences, walls and power lines, are excellent guides when they are marked on the map.

A route from control to control that makes use of guide-lines can be fast and relaxing for the competitor, for once he has aligned himself with an identified feature he can press on at speed for minutes on end.

In night orienteering the choice of a route would be heavily weighted by the existence of a guide-line, for when it is dark it is necessary to know where you are for every step of the way.

Collecting Features

Another use of obvious long-sided features is as 'collecting' devices. Often the problem of difficult navigation is not just one of travelling in the right direction but also of not going on too far. The experienced performer tends to pick a route which has collecting features straddled across the way. For instance, it can be quite safe to run hard across open heath land without too much finesse with compass and map, if the runner knows that he will be collected at a certain point by a boundary fence or a stream.

It is possible to traverse many of the legs of a course by means of linking together collecting features, and where this is possible it means that some fast, relaxed running can be done.

Aiming-off

A control is sometimes placed on or near a feature that has length—such as a stream, a lake or a path. The approach to such a control is often at right angles to the feature and across diffi-cult terrain. In such cases, it is not enough just to be collected

ORIENTEERING

by the feature, for it is essential to know on which side of the control you have arrived.

For instance, the stream in the forest that collects you after a traverse through the trees has the control on its bank. You know that you are out perhaps only 80 metres at the most in your dead reckoning—but which way should you turn first, upstream or down? A wrong choice could lose several minutes.

It is in this circumstance that the clever orienteer uses the 'aiming-off' technique. Instead of taking a compass bearing directly on to the control during the last half mile to the stream, he aims-off 100 metres or so upstream. Then when he hits the water he knows that the control must lie downstream and turns confidently that way. (*See* Figure 17.)

FIGURE 17

Aiming-off
The stream is deliberately hit to the west
of the control point.

This technique, although it does mean that a little extra distance is covered, is well worth adopting and does show a bonus when adopted throughout a race. For exact reckoning is very rare and even an error of 4° on a bearing across one grid square produces nearly 100 metres of discrepancy. This distance easily exceeds the limit of visibility in the forest.

ORIENTEERING

Speed must be expected to produce small errors; aiming-off will establish the direction of the inexactitude.

Determining Distances

More mistakes are made in orienteering by wrongly estimating distance than from any other reason. After a little experience most orienteers can manage to travel in the right direction; what they find hard to do is to know how far they have gone.

It is never entirely safe to rely on features other than those depicted by contours, so that whenever man-made features are being used for intermediate checks on a route, it is necessary to confirm their actuality by accurate distance checking. This is particularly true of paths, for they tend to come and go with a rapidity that the map-maker can never hope to approach.

The most efficient way of judging distance is by 'step-counting', and all experienced orienteers know precisely how many double-strides they take to cover 100 metres at a moderate trot on a particular surface. When it comes to counting steps it is far easier and relaxing to count every other stride.

The determining of distance by counting 'double-steps', e.g. one count for every time the left foot comes to the ground, is not new to the British scene. In fact, our national unit of distance—the mile, comes from the Roman soldiers' vocabulary. His thousand paces, the *mille passus* in Latin, were counted in pairs and the phrase came to be shortened to a 'mile'. Incidentally, this distance also produces the figure 5,280 for the number of feet in a mile, for this was the number of 'foot-lengths' of an average legionnaire in a *mille passus*.

It is quite simple to obtain a personal figure for the number of steps in 100 metres. Either the distance can be measured on the ground or the nearest athletic track can be used. In the case of the track, which will be 440 yards, near enough 400 metres, it is best to run at orienteering speed round the whole track and divide the figure by four. A fit runner will find that his left foot will strike the ground about thirty-five times every 100 metres. For the slower performer a figure nearer forty-two will be more appropriate. With practice and experience similar figures can be obtained for travel in rougher conditions.

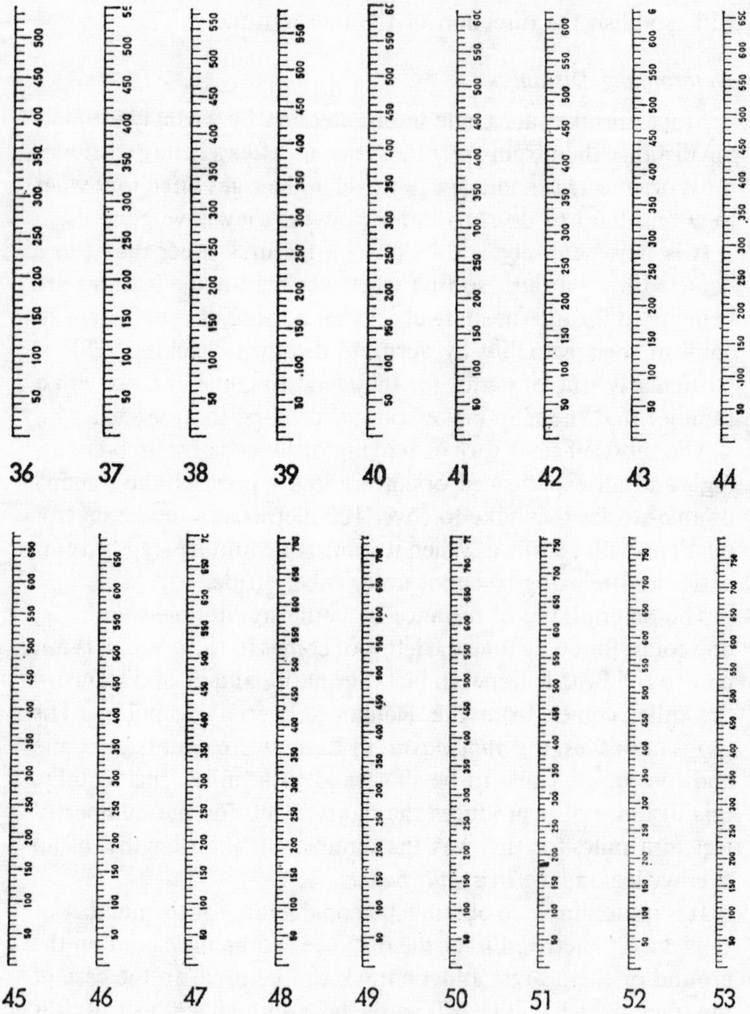

FIGURE 18

The Double-Step Scale

The various scales are for different speeds as determined over 100 metres, from the fast rate of 36 double-steps to the gentle speed of 53 double-steps for the 100 metres.

ORIENTEERING

Step-counting can become almost second nature to the orienteer; every time he leaves an identifiable point he starts counting. When things don't fall into place he stops and knows just how far he has progressed from the last known point. Paradoxically, the efficient orienteer knows where he is when he is lost.

The ultimate sophistication for the orienteer is to stop thinking in terms of metres and progress to converting distance into 'steps'. Instead of calculating that it is 230 metres to the next bend in the path he thinks that it is ninety steps away. To reduce the calculating process by one stage it is possible to devise a scale which measures distance on the 1 : 25,000 map in terms of steps. This scale can be stuck on the front edge of the base plate of the compass and used just like a ruler.

For your convenience a step scale for several different rates of progress is produced twice in this book, so it will be possible to cut out the scale that suits you and fix it to the leading edge of your Silva compass. The width of the scales is chosen with reference to the base plate of the Type 4 compass. For the narrower models all that is necessary to make the scale fit is to trim the right-hand edge of the slip.

'. . . marker flags should be hanging free at head height.'

6

Types of Orienteering Competition

Apart from the various minor 'training' games which can be used for preparation for orienteering proper, there are two major forms of the competitive sport. These are 'Score Orienteering' and 'Cross-Country Orienteering' events, with the latter type being the highest form of the sport and that used in International competition.

Both these forms of the game can be played at night as well as by day, and also used as the basis of a Relay competition.

There is also Line Orienteering, which although it is an excellent game is difficult to adapt to large numbers.

Score Orienteering

In this type of event a large number of control points, between twelve and twenty, are selected in an area of about three miles square. A points value is given to each control. Those controls on the periphery of the area or in situations difficult to locate are awarded high marks, perhaps 30–50 points, while controls near to the start (the finish is at the same point) would earn only 5–10 points for a visit.

The object of the game is for the competitor to visit, in any order he chooses, as many controls as possible within a given time limit, and so amass as large a total of points as possible. The period of time allowed can vary from race to race but is usually about 1½ hours. There is an abundance of controls, more than can possibly be harvested in the time given. To further encourage accurate pace and time judgement there is a penalty-point system which operates should the allowed time be exceeded. This penalty can be as high as 1 point deducted for every 10 seconds that the competitor is overdue at the finish. So a runner who arrives back at the finish some 6½ minutes late, will have 39 points deducted from his hard-won total.

The winner is the competitor who finishes with the highest score—corrected if necessary with respect to lateness. There is, of course, no reward for arriving at the finish with time in hand, for the object of this exercise is to use up every minute allowed to the best possible advantage.

Score Events offer some advantages over other forms of orienteering.

1. They can be held in reasonably open country, for as the linking together of the controls is a matter of personal preference there is not likely to be a procession formed as when the orienteers all move in the same pattern of progress. This means that fairly open park land can be used without good visibility detracting from the enjoyment of the event.

2. Competitors of all standards can compete together in the same event. The stronger performers can cover 6–8 miles in 90 minutes, while the novices, women and juniors can complete the event to their own standards, probably covering 3 to 4 miles in the time allowed.

3. The event can be confined to a comparatively short period of time. A 'flock' of competitors can be set off at the same time so that the whole entry can be started within half an hour. With a time limit set for the return most of the competitors will be within a 2-hour period. This means that fairly large meetings can be held in the summer evenings and even night events can be over in winter by nine o'clock.

General Conduct of a Score Event

At their appropriate start-time competitors are given the map and a score-sheet. The score-sheet lists and numbers all the Controls and indicates their respective points value. *See* page 140.

The Master Maps are dotted with red circles showing the sites of all the controls, which are numbered to correspond with the score-sheet description of the control. *See* Map 11. The competitor's first task is to copy all the red circles on to his own map; as there could be up to twenty of these signs this job could take at least 6 to 8 minutes.

With this information collected, the orienteer must now devise an economic and productive circuit around as many of the controls as possible, remembering that he has only a certain period of time available.

He will notice that the controls farthest away offer the greatest reward and there will be others which are buried deep in pathless country which also promise high dividends. It is not likely that everyone will select the same pattern of collection as anyone else, but all the good orienteers will have followed certain sensible rules.

1. A route out to the perimeter should pass by as many controls as possible, and similarly the journey home should be productive.

2. Several controls near to the finish should be left ungathered on the way out. This will mean that should the run for home bring the competitor back too early, then the spare minutes can be used profitably.

This pre-running brain work takes time to do properly. Four to five minutes spent in intelligent plotting can equal several miles of leg-work and separate the tortoises from the hares. In some events, particularly where there are a number of novices competing, the organizer insists that a full 15 minutes are spent in the Master Map area. This ensures that no one is panicked into sudden flight before they have devised a suitable route. In such a case there would be about 6 minutes available for study after the details had been copied from the Master Map.

Team Competition

Team competition can be arranged in two ways in Score events. Firstly, as in any other orienteering event, the results of the best members of a team can be added together to produce a total. In senior events the usual regulations state 'that up to eight members can be nominated and five shall count for the team'. For juniors and women, nominations are often five and three count for the prize.

1. The author

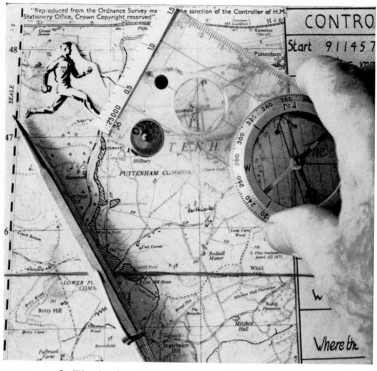

2. The basic equipment needed by the orienteer

3. Master-maps set up on trestles in the forest for a school's competition

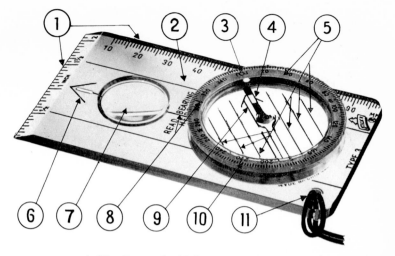

4. *The Parts of a 'Silva' Type 3 Compass*

1. Scales: in inches, centimetres and millimetres. 2. Base plate (transparent). 3. North point of dial (luminous). 4. Magnetic needle (liquid-dampened with north end red and luminous). 5. Compass housing with dial and orienting lines. 6. Direction-of-travel arrow. 7. Magnifying lens. 8. Index pointer. 9. Orienting arrow. 10. Graduated dial —360° in 2-degree graduations. 11. Safety cord

5. Lieutenant Griffiths, representing Scotland, at the master maps during an event for the Services in Sweden

6. Completely absorbed, two boys work out their salvation during a London Federation of Boys' Clubs race

7. A girl competitor, her hair protected from tree branches, sets her map at a control point

8. A competitor at a night control

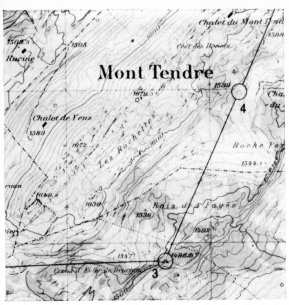

9. (TOP) : A section of the Swiss map for the 1964 World Championship. Control 3 is 'on the rocks' and No. 4 is 'in the niche'. The best time recorded between these two controls was seven minutes. Contours are ten metres apart

10. (BOTTOM) : A section of a Swedish map for the Sweden–Denmark competition in 1963. The best times between the first four controls were 16 min., 4 min., 10 min. and 5 min. respectively. Contours are five metres apart

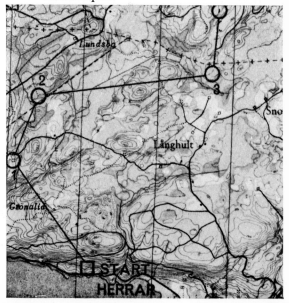

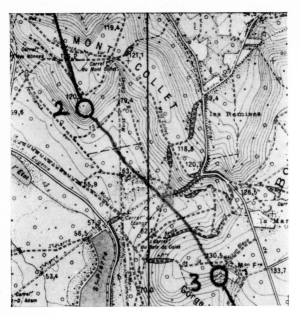

11. A section of the French map for an international event in 1965. The control circles and joining lines are those made by the competitor at the master-maps. Note this excellent example of an 'across or round' problem. Contours are five metres apart

12. By the light of head torches, senior men competitors copy down information on to their maps from the instruction sheets

13. Chris Brasher, Chairman of the British Orienteering Federation moves away from a control point on the edge of the Surrey Downs

14. Two competitors take the opportunity of replacing sugar and salt at a 'food station'. This was during a 14-mile event in Switzerland

15. Officials need to be as tough as the competitors. Here the recorder checks the control card of the finishing runner at the end of a winter's afternoon

ORIENTEERING

It is usual to consider the actual performance of each competitor in orienteering team races, rather than just taking note of his position in the results. This means that the various points totals will be added together to determine the team result in a Score event, the team with the highest combined score being the winner.

The second way of making a score event a team competition does not permit an individual result being calculated as well. In this case the team works together as a corporate body. At the start of the competition, when the master-map information has been copied, the leader of a team assigns various controls to each member. The strong runners would be asked to collect the far-flung controls while the weaker members would gather in the nearer points.

This form of team event is excellent where there is a great variation in the ability of members of the various teams, for everyone is playing a genuine part and occupied to the full extent of their potential. The expert and novice as well as men and women can be part of a joint enterprise.

Cross-Country Orienteering

Cross-country orienteering is the sport at its most competitive and intriguing best. Here, because all the competitors must visit the controls in the same order, there is a direct battle of wits and stamina. The rightness of a decision is directly reflected by the stop-watch. If going round a hill instead of over it was the correct course, then the time saved is credited in the overall time taken for the event.

Most events have between six to ten controls situated in undulating, well-wooded terrain, and courses vary in length from 3 miles for junior and novice events to 9 miles for senior championship events. The circuit can be a closed one, with the start and finish at the same point, or the finish can be several miles away from the point of departure.

The order that the controls must be visited is clearly indicated by the organizer and the winner is the competitor that circulates the course the fastest.

ORIENTEERING

The basic procedure taken by the competitor in a cross-country event has been described in Chapter 2, and further administration details will be found in the Chapter dealing with the organization of a race. The competent orienteer is not only good at competing but is also an expert at organizing an event, in fact, his success as a racer is directly due to his insight into the mind of the race organizer. It is a case of 'setting a thief to catch a thief'.

One of the most difficult areas of contact between competitor and organizer is that of verbal semantics—that is, making sure that the same word conveys the same meaning to both parties. To standardize the definition of the various features used as control points, the British Orienteering Federation has produced a 'Control Terminology' guide.

This official guide lists some fifty different situations and also indicates positively what various features should be called. The adoption of a standard terminology means that the competitor from any part of the country knows exactly what a word conveys. For instance, every competitor knows that the word 'knoll' indicates a piece of raised ground some 25–40 ft. higher than its surrounds, and that it is probably indicated by a 'ring-contour'.

Control Terminology and Definition of Features

1. Controls shall be marked on the Master Maps by RED circles of $\frac{1}{2}$ cm. in diameter. The situation of the control shall be in the exact middle of this circle—but *not* indicated by a dot.

2. When the control feature exists on the map as well as on the ground, then the brief verbal description of the site may include the 'definite article', e.g. '*The* track-end,' or '*The* footbridge'.

3. When the control feature exists on the ground but is not shown on the map, then the description shall include the 'indefinite article', e.g. 'A stile on the track', or 'A tall pine'.

4. A 'six-figure' map reference may be included in the designation of the control.

5. Controls shall be numbered on the Master Maps.

6. For cross-country events the controls shall be joined to-

gether on the Master Map by a red line, indicating the shape of the course.

(SEE MAP NO. 7, BETWEEN PAGES 48–49.)

Notes on Examples (Figures refer to the sample numbers in Maps 2 and 3)

1. The double line 'foot-path' is called a track.

5. The single-line 'foot-path' is called a path.

8. In the case of a junction between a marked-on-the-map track and an unindicated path the description would be: 'The track and a path junction.'

13. In Scotland or Wales, the words 'loch' or 'llyn' may be used in preference to the term 'lake'.

14. A 'pond' is a small area of water, i.e. about 25 yards across.

21. The unqualified use of the term 'summit' indicates that the actual top of the hill is obviously discernible.

22. Where the summit is a plateau, the actual site of the control must be indicated.

26. The use of the term 'ridge' indicates that the control is situated directly on the spine of the ridge.

27. A 'spur' is the term used for a minor ridge that erupts from a main ridge. It is often flanked by re-entrants.

28. The term 'neck' is applied to the crest of a hill where the high ground is pinched-in or waisted.

32. A minor side valley, off a main valley is called a 're-entrant'. (The word is not used here in its geographical context.)

33. A 'knoll' will usually be indicated by a single ring-contour on the map.

35. The term 'gap' is used to describe a narrow area between a knoll and a hill or another knoll.

36. A 'pulpit' is the term given to a small bulge extruding from a hillside. It would normally be indicated on the map by a kink in a single contour.

37. The term 'niche' is used to describe the hollow in a hillside slope. On a map it is indicated by an indent in a single contour.

42. The one symbol on the map indicating a 'boundary' covers

all the words—fence, hedge, wall, ditch and dyke (a dyke is a raised mound with a ditch one side of it). After the term 'boundary' the type of the barrier should be indicated.

43. A 'field' is enclosed by boundaries, and will be growing a crop—grass is also a crop.

44. A 'clearing' is an unfenced area found in forests and will be treeless and about 40 yards square at least.

45-48. The points of the compass are used to indicate which side of a feature is used as the control site. Where there is more than one 'point', the word 'most' should be added.

49. Many other features require no further explanation than reference to the Conventional Signs: Trig. point, footbridge, tumulus, well, spring, quarry, etc. These terms stand on their own, only the 'definite' article (the) needs to be added—where it is correct so to do.

Night Orienteering

After dark, orienteering is a very sophisticated game indeed and demands a high level of skill for successful participation. There is little opportunity for the novice to learn as he goes along in a night event and consequently this form of the sport is best suited for the experienced competitor.

The two basic skills—those of direction finding and distance judging are at full stretch in a night event. Hardly a step can be taken without the compass being consulted and the stride counted. So many of the day-time 'guide lines' are lost to sight when the circle of vision is reduced to fifteen yards. The edge of a clearing is an obvious feature in the day time; at night it is just another area of blackness, perhaps a little lighter than the surrounding night, but by no means a pointer for direction.

This increase in the difficulty factor makes it possible to use quite domestic areas of terrain for night events—commons and parks, too open or cramped for normal competition, are often ideal for use after dark. A very successful event was recently held on part of Wimbledon Common, only 8 miles from the centre of London. Even though most of the entrants admitted to being familiar with the area there was a high ratio of non-finishers. Actually, only twenty seniors completed the $3\frac{1}{4}$-mile course out of the sixty or so who started, while the average time taken by the best ten competitors was a tardy 100 minutes. As this produces an average speed of 30 minutes for each mile, it will be appreciated that navigational problems were high. Nearly every competitor underestimated the desert-like quality of a common at night. Landmarks were scarce, while the general proliferation of paths made this feature a hopeless peg on which to hang an estimate of position once lost. Lack of fences and buildings added to the difficulty of 'starting again' from a known identifiable spot.

This, of course, is the secret of success in night orienteering—never a step should be taken unless its worth is confirmed by all the available evidence.

The night-orienteer tends to be overdressed by daytime standards. Because it is colder at night and the level of physical exercise lower, the competitor will be well advised to wear several layers of clothes on his upper body and long pants on his legs. A tough nylon anorak gives good protection against the weather and unseen tree branches. Lightweight boots are better than cross-country shoes or gym shoes, for the torch does not always pick out the pot-hole in the path or the hidden stump of tree in the bracken.

The best kind of torch is a headlamp, as used by cavers. This produces a broad band of light from a source that doesn't dazzle the eyes and also leaves the hands completely free to hold the map and manipulate the compass. Only those who have tried will appreciate the difficulty of taking a bearing from the map with a compass while the torch is held between the teeth!

Whatever torch is used it should have large batteries. The newcomer to night racing seldom appreciates that the torch is used continuously for perhaps two hours on end. Few single-cell batteries can survive such treatment and night navigation is difficult enough without the added handicap of an ailing torch. Personally I not only use a torch which incorporates a large long-life battery but I also carry a new spare battery as well. Should I fall and break the bulb then I have a spare replacement for that item of equipment too.

ORIENTEERING

One further advantage of the head torch is that it is far enough away from the compass needle not to affect its correct alignment. Many hand torches greatly disturb the needle when held close to the compass, consequently, if you have to use a hand torch make sure it is a plastic model.

Safety

The organizer of a night event needs to be safety-minded. This means that first and foremost he must select an area for the competition that is hazardless, and certainly free of deep rivers, cliffs and quarries. Controls should be fairly close together and the area contained within easily recognizable features, such as roads or high fences.

In the interests of safety all the competitors will carry whistles, which will only be used in case of emergency or as a signal that the controls are being collected by the organizer. The noise of a whistle carries much better than the voice and is also more durable if help has to be summoned for some time. The Rules of the British Orienteering Federation state that a whistle is a compulsory item of equipment for all starters in a night event.

The B.O.F. also specifies that all those in the Boys and Girls class, and the Junior women, must compete as pairs or groups in night events.

These regulations may seem to be rather arbitrary at first acquaintance but anyone who has been involved in a night event when the weather turns rough will at once endorse their necessity. A pitch-dark night with lashing rain is a salutary experience for an adult and too hard a lesson for a solitary junior to enjoy.

Controls

The site of the control in a night event is generally on a specific feature which can be identified with precision. Many of the excellent places that can be used in daytime are completely unsuitable for the hours of darkness. For instance, although the spine of a ridge or the floor of a valley is readily located in daytime, at night they are extremely difficult to find. The light of a torch can seldom distinguish a minor bump in the ground from a major change of slope.

Therefore, at night, controls are located at the junctions of paths or tracks that are marked on the map, or on a footbridge over a stream. The good control in a night event is one that can almost be identified by touch.

The actual marker used can be the normal 'flag' but, to help attract the attention just a little bit more, a lamp can be used as well. Very little light is needed, too much will certainly make it too easy to see the area from hundreds of yards away. Even a red road-lamp gives too much light, unless it is enclosed in an up-ended oil drum or cardboard box. An alternative marker which makes much less work for the course setter is one which is painted with fluorescent red paint. The Southern Orienteering Association uses plaques of white Formica 12 inches square, painted with the red paint used by sign-writers. These markers glow brightly when even the faintest beam of light shines on them.

Types of Night Event

Both major forms of orienteering are suitable for night competition. Cross-country events should not exceed 5 miles for senior competition.

Score events are perhaps the better type of competition for after-dark races. They have the advantage in that there is never a procession formed by the torches as they go from control to control because there are dozens of different ways of linking the points together. Secondly, the time factor in a Score event has the effect of encouraging competitors to return promptly to the finish within a reasonable time and preferably before the nearby hotel shuts.

Relay Racing

The relay race is always popular with club members and it can be used in orienteering with as much success as it is in athletics.

In Sweden the largest competition of the year is the '10-milakavlen' event (the Swedish mile is worth six English ones). This is an inter-club contest where 100 clubs enter teams of ten runners each. The race continues all through one night, with each runner negotiating some 5–8 miles of terrain, and lasts about 15 hours.

The great advantage of the relay race is that every member of the team is equally important to the corporate success of the venture. This makes relay racing extremely valuable to the school and youth scene, where often the weaker performer finds little incentive to try his hardest. Personal motivation doesn't get as much out of the average performer as does group enthusiasm, so that the stimulus of relays often works wonders with the half-hearted or half-fit performer.

The Clover Leaf Relay

From a central control point several leaves can radiate out to give courses for each 'leg' of the race. By having the change-

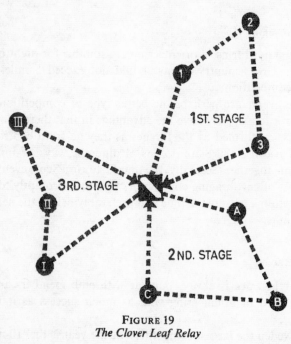

FIGURE 19
The Clover Leaf Relay

over points at one location the administration of such a race is made relatively easy, as there is no transport of competitors to complicate the issue.

The various legs of the relay will be out and back courses and can all be three or four controls long. However, legs of varying difficulty could be devised to suit the composition of the teams concerned—'Courses for horses'. Mixed teams could be catered for by such an arrangement, or ones of varying ages.

The starting sequence of a relay race can be at 2 or 3-minute intervals as in a normal cross-country event. The master-map for the first runners need only show the controls of the first leg of the race. The subsequent runners will only be able to start when their predecessor arrives back at the start.

Some kind of 'baton'—a disc on a cord that can be worn around the neck should be used, or the map itself can be used as the baton. This latter method has the advantage of reducing the number of maps needed for the competition.

'Out and Back' and 'Point to Point' Relays

With rather more officials and organization problems it is possible to have several different 'change-over' points, so that the race is over a circular course or starts and finishes several miles apart.

Rules

All the normal rules and regulations concerning cross-country orienteering will apply to Relay orienteering. One further rule is laid down by the B.O.F: 'A competitor is only allowed to run one stage.'

Line Orienteering

This fascinating form of orienteering is very interesting for fairly experienced performers but can only be done successfully with fairly long intervals between each competitor. Consequently, only small groups can compete with satisfaction in an event.

The competitors follow on the ground a line marked only on the master-map. If they succeed in exactly following the course indicated by the line on the map, they will pass by a number of controls. As there is no indication on the master-maps of the situation of these controls or the number of them, great precision is needed throughout the course. (*See* Map 6.)

This will mean that there is no choice of routes between controls in a Line event and that all the competitors will be, unless they make a mistake, following in each others' footsteps. Hence, there needs to be a fairly long interval between each starter and this will, of course, reduce the effective size of the entry.

As in cross-country orienteering the winner is the one who visits all the controls in the fastest time. The control stations are clearly numbered in the order, 1, 2, 3, etc., so that the competitor can at once see if he has missed a control in his circuit. He may then decide to retrace the previous section of the route, or continue on to the finish. The organizer sets a time penalty for 'missed' controls, and this will depend upon the length and difficulty of the course. In a normal event, perhaps 15–20 minutes would be a reasonable penalty for every control not found.

A Line course can pass along tracks and paths, the boundaries of woods, streams, and also across in a straight line from feature to feature. The markers are spread out around this course at about the same interval as they would be in a cross-country event.

A Line event becomes a battle of wits between the competitor and the course-setter, with the experienced orienteer trying to predict where the next control is likely to be set. It is fairly obvious that the controls are going to be placed where their position siting cannot be disputed. This will mean that identifiable features will be used, or spots where back-bearings make positioning certain. Working on this rationalization of the problem, the experienced line-orienteer will be slow and careful at some sections of the course, and fast and less precise at others.

The Code of Conduct

Pair and group participation in orienteering is an acceptable and necessary aid to the learning process, as well as, in the case of night events, often essential for safety's sake.

ORIENTEERING

However, groups larger than three are to be greatly discouraged, as a unit of four or more often becomes a crowd—noisy and out of character with the event.

From an early stage newcomers to the sport should be encouraged to regard orienteering as an intensely personal skill, which owes nothing to outside help. The quality of the 'Pimpernel' should be in every orienteer's heart—to see and not be seen. No serious competitor seeks advice or gives it to another, neither does he wish to be led to a control position by the chatter or shouts of other participants.

The good orienteer spends as little time as possible close to the control flag; as soon as he has stamped his card, he quietly moves away so that his movements or clothing do not attract others to the site. The rules make special reference to clothing in this one context. 'No red clothing should be worn'. In fact, dark colours that make the competitor as unobtrusive as possible are the best for orienteering.

There is little doubt that once a person has been exposed to the competitive nature of the game he becomes as 'damned elusive' as possible to other competitors. There are plenty of incidents where ditch and hedge have been used to conceal one competitor while one of his rivals passes by still searching for the control.

Two other aspects of social awareness must be well appreciated by the orienteer.

1. *Respect of private property*. The fact that a competitor is in a race does not make him invulnerable to the laws of trespass, or entitle him to ignore the Country Code.

Orienteering can only take place with the co-operation of landowners, and for many organizers the success of a race will be judged on whether it is possible to return to the venue again. Broken fence rails, trampled corn and frightened animals will hardly make a return visit welcome.

Whenever the organizer indicates that a certain area is 'out-of-bounds' he does so for the best of reasons. He will be well advised to disqualify outright anyone who ignores his instructions.

2. *Consideration to the organizer*. Once a competitor has been

checked out at the start of a race, it is essential for the organizer's peace of mind that he knows that the competitor has returned to the finish. This is the 'first commandment' of orienteering and it must be obeyed whether the course is completed or not. If for some reason or other, the competitor cannot physically report to the finish, then he should personally make sure that a responsible message reaches the race organizer to this effect.

Search parties are unpopular with tired orienteers at the best of times, but wild-goose chases are even more to be deplored.

For further endorsement of the above section of the book, Rules 29–34 should be read of the 'Rules of Competition'. (*See* Chapter 10.)

'. . . *the orienteer attempts to avoid leading other competitors to a control.*'

7

Practical Training Games for Orienteering

Miniature Score Event

A great deal of fun and instruction can be obtained in a limited area by using large-scale plans or maps. A scale as large as 1 inch to 100 yards, or the Ordnance Survey 6 inches to 1 mile, shows the ground plan of every building as well as paths, fences, etc.

Most beginners find it easy to set a map in relation with a building, so that the more structures there are in the area used the better. A university campus would be ideal, with many buildings set in parkland. Once the novice has been shown how to set a map by 'squaring' it off with an identifiable building he can navigate around such a site with confidence and without a compass.

With numbers of school-class size and a limited time available, the teacher or youth leader will find that a simple 'score' event will be the most successful way of introducing the activity.

Controls can be indicated by discreet postcard-size markers and points can be awarded to each control just as in a full-size competition. A time limit of 15 minutes will hardly give the most talented performer time to cover more than about a mile of collecting.

Route Orienteering

For this practice a course is marked out on the ground with coloured streamers, so that the route can be seen and followed by competitors. Along this course a number of control markers are placed, and when the novice comes across these he is asked to mark on his map exactly where he thinks he has reached.

Courses can be a couple of miles long and as there is no danger of anyone losing the way the event is suitable for the young and inexperienced.

As the competitor follows the streamers across the terrain he also has to estimate his progress on the map, and this makes the game an excellent practice for precise reckoning and careful observation.

The game is made competitive by asking the competitors to complete the circuit as quickly as possible, and also setting a penalty for any error in estimating the position of the various controls passed *en route*.

For instance, two minutes could be added on to the competitor's time for every $\frac{1}{16}$ in. error in the placing of a dot indicating the position of a control.

A Point orienteering course should pass through as many fixed points as possible in the area, such as path junctions, hilltops, streams and lakes, so that the competitor has many opportunities of re-confirming his position on the map. At the site of a control the competitor can estimate his position by use of the map alone. If compasses are available this exercise is ideal as an encouragement to practise back-bearing techniques.

Compass Practices

Successful use of a protractor-type compass, such as the Silva model, depends upon two factors:

1. That the eye is directly over the needle—so that its position can be precisely gauged.

2. That the compass is held at right angles to the body directly in front of the chest—so that the head and eyes are directly in line with the direction-of-travel arrow.

A simple group practice can be done on a school soccer pitch by taking bearings on a central flag from the corners and half-way points of the field. The results can be checked by the leader —perhaps by using a prismatic compass. (*See* Figure 20.)

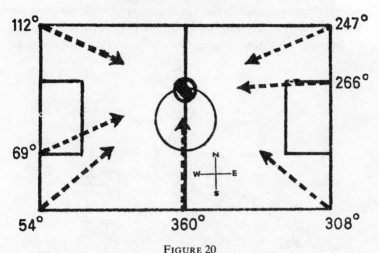

FIGURE 20

Bearing practice, using a soccer pitch

Travel on a Bearing

The secret of accurate travel on a compass bearing is never to move when looking at the compass. Once the needle is steady over the orienting arrow, the eyes are raised and an object found in the direct line of vision. This selected object, perhaps a tree or bank of earth, is kept clearly in view, and without further resort to the compass it is run towards.

It is inaccurate and dangerous to proceed with the head down trying to keep the needle steady. In fact, it is not often appreciated that it is possible to always keep the needle exactly aligned and still be degrees off course while moving, if you walk crab-wise.

Again it is possible to use a marked pitch to practise walking on a bearing. Previously determined bearings and distances can be worked out to provide a circuit around and across the pitch. Students trace their route on a piece of paper and compare the result with the master-sheet prepared by the leader.

Hunt the Silver Dollar

Accurate compass work, precise step counting and an appre-ciation of the degrees in a circle can be developed by the game

d 'Hunt the Silver Dollar'. A small object is put down at the
, such as a silver milk bottle top, then a course is paced out
bearings. A three-sided figure is best to start with and legs

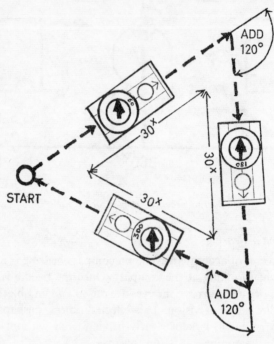

FIGURE 21
Hunt the Silver Dollar

should be about 20 yards long. Any bearing can be selected for
the first side of the triangle; at the end of the paced distance 120
degrees are added to the first bearing and similarly at the second
corner another 120 degrees are added. Accurate work should
bring the traveller back exactly over the 'dollar'. (*See* Figure 21.)

A progression can be made to a square or five- or six-sided
figure. The added angle in each case is obtained by dividing the
number of sides of the figure into 360 degrees.

Miniature Orienteering

In this game the student travels from control to control

following instructions as to bearing to be followed and how far
to proceed.

Any area well supplied with trees can be used for miniature
orienteering. A dozen or so controls are laid out in the area and
information provided on the 'flags' to link the course together.
(*See* Figure 22.)

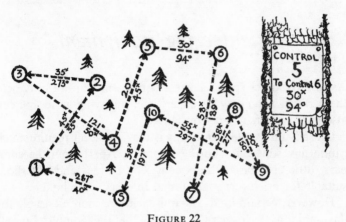

FIGURE 22

A Miniature Orienteering Course
A course can be set up in any well-wooded area.

The course can have a separate start and finish, or for the
purposes of training be a continuous circuit so that any control
can be used as a starting point. By using the latter method it is
possible to get a class working quickly, always an important
consideration in a teaching situation.

'. . . *a water-proof watch is useful.*'

8

Orienteering Equipment

As in most other sports, correct equipment can not only help the performer to enjoy the experience of playing more, but can also improve personal performance.

One advantage of orienteering is that it doesn't require much capital investment in sports equipment. Apart from the compass, little else has to be bought. Old clothes and old shoes suitable for orienteering are found in every household.

However, certain kinds of equipment are more desirable for the ambitious performer than others, and the 'complete' orienteer is going to possess specialist gear before he has been competing for long.

Clothing

The body needs to be protected against the weather and also against abrasion caused by tree branches, bracken and brambles. The clothing needs to cover all the body and be light and loose enough to facilitate active movement.

Ideally, knitted nylon material makes the best garments for orienteers, as the garments are light in weight, the polished surface of the material does not easily snag on thorns, and it dries quickly after wetting (or washing).

Tee shirt needs to be loose fitting, have long sleeves and a collar and a breast-pocket, 9 in. wide and 6 in. deep. The pocket should be protected by a flap, and closed by a 'rip' type fastening.

Trousers need to be of a track-suit pattern with tapered legs and ankle fastenings, and have a zip-fastened hip pocket.

Running vest and shorts made of cotton should be worn under the outer garments. In winter a long-sleeved wool jersey should also be worn under the shirt.

Stockings. Long football-type stockings which further protect the front of the lower leg against damage are worn by most serious competitors. In fact, in Sweden it is possible to buy a stocking which has a pad stitched into the front of it, so that a bramble ripping across the front of the leg does no damage at all.

Footwear. Although gym shoes can be suitable for easy terrain, some support for the ankle is essential in rough country.

One of the best types of boot is a canvas hockey boot with rubber studs in the sole. This lightweight boot gives protection and rigidity to the ankle and good grip on muddy surfaces. Some makes have bars on the sole rather than studs; this type is not so good, as the bars tend to slide on greasy traverses.

For fast, dry courses, cross-country running shoes are excellent.

Compass

Only one type of instrument makes sense to the orienteer and that is the one that combines the properties of a compass and a protractor.

Today the word 'SILVA' is practically synonymous with the phrase 'protractor-type compass', and the Swedish firm Ab Bröderna Kjellström who manufacture the 'SILVA' compass are closely linked with the sport of orienteering. The English distributor for 'SILVA' compasses is B. J. Ward Ltd., and this firm imports several different models which are designed not only for the orienteer but for any traveller in rough or mountainous country.

Three models in particular are designed especially for the orienteer. They are all protractor-type instruments. The baseplates have a magnifying lens let into them and are marked out as a ruler in inches and centimetres. The needle housing is graduated into 360° and luminous points on the dial and the needle make it possible for the compass to be read at night.

Type 5. This is the cheapest available model and costs 15s. 6d.

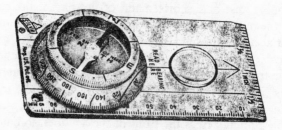

FIGURE 23

TYPE 5 SILVA JUNIOR

A simplified induction damped Silva System Compass. Official compass among Scouts, in schools and other youth organizations in many countries. Induced electricity forms to stop the needle swing.

Measurements of plate: 4″ × 2″—100 × 50 mm.

Weight: 1¾ oz—45 g.

Marking of compass points and alternative graduations:
Type: 5/360.
NESW 360°.
Short scale in $\frac{1}{16}$ inches; Long scale in mm.

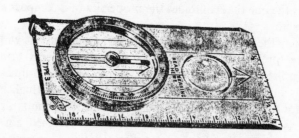

TYPE 3 EXPLORER III

A popular priced quality compass with all the above mentioned Silva features. The improved model with magnifying lens has in one year become tremendously popular.

Measurements of plate: 4″ × 2⅛″—100 × 54 mm.

Weight: 1½ oz.—37 g.

Marking of compass points and alternative graduations:
Type: 3/360.
NESW 360°.
Short scale in $\frac{1}{16}$ inches; Long scale in mm.

100

ORIENTEERING

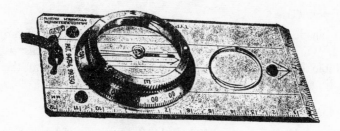

TYPE 1 EXPLORER

A high quality compass for the exacting user with all 'Silva' features and with a sturdy dial of aluminium.

Measurement of plate: 5″ × 2⅜″—125 × 60 mm.

Weight: 2 oz.—52 g.

Marking of compass points and alternative graduations:
Type: 1/360, 1/6400, 1/4 × 90.
NESW 360°, 6400' or 4 × 90°.
Short scale in 1/16 inches; Long scale in mm.

from sports shops, or 16s. postage paid from B. J. Ward Ltd., 130 Westminster Bridge Road, London, S.E.1.

The needle housing is not transparent, so the orienting lines are marked on the rim. This makes it a little slower to use as a protractor than the other models—but no less accurate if care is taken. The needle is damped in its swing by induced electricity. The base-plate is 4 in. × 2 in.

Type 3. This is a new all-plastic model (apart from the steel needle) with an easy-to-read scale on the needle-housing rim. It is a very attractive proposition for the average orienteer at 28s. 6d. (29s. post inc.). This compass is a delight to handle and accurate to use at speed. The base-plate size is 4 in. × 2⅛ in.

Type 1. This larger and heavier (2 oz.) compass has a base-plate 5 in. × 2⅜ in. and is the choice of most serious and competitive orienteers. Although it is relatively expensive at 53s. 6d. (54s. post inc.), its robustness makes it a lifetime buy.

The base-plate and needle housing are made of shatter-proof plastic and the needle swings on sapphire bearings. The whole product is a fine piece of precision engineering.

ORIENTEERING

Compass Case

A plastic compass case with a press-stud flap is available from B. J. Ward Ltd., price 3s. 6d. including postage. The case is suitable for all orienteering compasses and will prevent the plastic surface becoming scratched and spoilt.

Tachometer

This small gadget is a 'clicker' that registers digits from 0–9. It is screwed on to the base plate of the compass and is used as an *aide-mémoire* for the competitive orienteer when he is step counting.

It can be bought already fitted on to a Type 1 or 3 compass, and adds 10s. 6d. to the cost. Bought as a separate item from B. J. Ward, Ltd., it costs 9s. 6d., postage paid.

Map Case

A simple plastic bag has certain limitations as a map-case, for it does not give a firm, flat surface. Such a surface is needed for a compass to rest on when bearings are being calculated. Consequently, heavy gauge clear plastic is needed, and this comes ready for use from office equipment shops. The standard foolscap plastic file cover, costing about 1s., is perfect for orienteering purposes. The map and other pieces of paper slot into the case and can be easily read when inside. For travelling the case can be rolled into a cylinder and carried in the hand.

Watch

A wrist-watch is essential for Score Events and useful for all orienteering races. It is possible to buy an underwater diver's watch with a rotating 'bezel' for about £5–£8. This watch is ideal for the orienteer for it will survive the worst thunderstorm and the bezel makes the calculation of elapsed time very easy.

Headlamp

An excellent 'caver's' lamp is available at a cost of 19s. 6d. from some sports shops. It is called the 'Achil' lamp and consists of two sources of light—one fitted on the forehead and the other carried in the hand or fixed on the belt. It is marketed by P.T.C. Ltd., Dorking, Surrey, and available from 'Pindisports', 14, Holborn, London, E.C.1.

Control Markers

It is not yet possible to buy these 'flags' from any source in England, and so all the ones in use are 'home-made'.

A suitable material to make control markers is 12 oz. canoe canvas; it is rot-proof and dyed bright red in colour. It is sold by the yard (about 11s. 6d.) and is 36 in. wide.

Simple 'flags' can be made out of this material and if they are 24 in. × 18 in. in size, the cost of six markers will be about 25s. for the material.

A much better marker is one which does not present an end-on view from any angle. Cylinder-shaped markers can be made fairly easily but need twice as much canvas for each marker.

Details of the construction of markers are given in Figure 24.

Marking Stamps

These Swedish-made stamps are self-inking and appear to keep giving a clear mark for years.

A set of ten different letters costs 60s., or five for 30s., and are obtainable from B. J. Ward Ltd.

Maps

For most types of races the orienteer is always concerned with the Ordnance Survey 1: 25,000 map. This series covers nearly all of Great Britain; only parts of northern Scotland are missing.

This map is seldom available in a local stationery shop, but it can be ordered through the Official Ordnance Survey agents who are to be found in most large towns. Only educational establishments requiring maps for educational purposes can order them direct from The Director General, Ordnance Survey, Chessington, Surrey.

Schools and colleges involved in orienteering as part of their general programme can benefit by ordering direct from the O.S., to the extent of 33⅓ per cent discount. This will reduce the cost

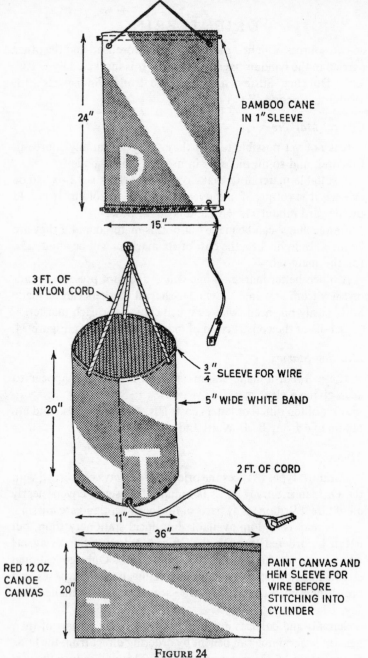

BAMBOO CANE IN 1" SLEEVE

24"

15"

3 FT. OF NYLON CORD

3/4" SLEEVE FOR WIRE

5" WIDE WHITE BAND

20"

2 FT. OF CORD

11"

36"

RED 12 OZ. CANOE CANVAS

20"

PAINT CANVAS AND HEM SLEEVE FOR WIRE BEFORE STITCHING INTO CYLINDER

FIGURE 24
Control Markers
(Design and Construction)

of a single coloured, paper, flat sheet from 5s. 6d. to 3s. 8d., not including postage.

To order a 1:25,000 scale map sheet the following information is needed.

1. Scale and Series: 1:25,000 National Grid.

2. Sheet Number: the Sheet borders coincide with the accentuated 10-kilometre grid lines on the 1-in. map, the sheet number being the grid reference of the S.W. corner to two figures only. For example: T Q—Grid letters from lower margin of a 1-in. map. 1—First figure of Easting line 10; 7—First figure of Northing line 70, produces *T Q* 17.

3. Edition: Coloured.

4. Style: Paper, flat.

The use of original maps makes practical orienteering a fairly expensive affair. However, a school or college using the same area for training purposes month after month may find that an original map covered with 'CONTACT' or some other transparent adhesive plastic is an economic proposition. A particular course can be marked on the map before it is sealed with the plastic, and then it can be used time and time again by students. Additional marks and lines can be drawn on the surface of the plastic with certain 'fibreglass-nib' pens and cleaned off after use.

Copier Machines and Reproductions

For the vast majority of orienteering races a good quality cheap reproduction of a map is all that is needed.

The recent advent of the 'dyeline' and other copying techniques has made this a practical proposition, and most organizers use such methods to obtain cheap black and white maps.

The machines that do the copying are expensive and only found in large business offices. However, the close connection between physical education and youth officers has happily enabled many county halls to lend the use of their machines for orienteering purposes. Similar machines are also available at airports and some large railway stations, where a foolscap copy costs 2s. This makes the cost of the map rather high, unless two maps can be reproduced on the same page, bringing the price down to 1s. a copy.

ORIENTEERING

The most often found machine is the 'Rank Xerox 914 Copier'. It produces excellent quality results at about 4d. for a foolscap copy. A further reduction in this cost can be obtained by printing a 'plate' in the Copier machine, and then using the plate to produce duplicated copies on a 'Rotaprint' machine. This second machine churns off copies for just the cost of the paper.

The Rank machine has, like most of the other copier machines, a colour blindness—in this case it is blue. The map original must be prepared to meet this failing and all streams and other bodies of water inked-in with black ink or ball-point pen. To avoid confusion with contours, streams and rivers are usually over-marked with a wiggly line, and lakes are banded.

One other fault is noticeable on close inspection; it is that the copy is about 1 per cent larger than the original. This exaggeration of 1 metre in a hundred is small enough to be ignored, and as the enlargement is in all directions, the accuracy of bearings is not affected.

Rank Limited provides a copying service in London, Birmingham, Manchester, Newcastle-on-Tyne and in Glasgow. They will reproduce at 9d. a copy, orders of 100 or more, using the 'electro-static' method as practised on the 914 machine. If more than four days' notice can be given, the company will be able to use the 'off-set' plate technique. The cost of 100 copies by this method is 25s., including the cost of the prepared plate that they make from the original map. (*See* Appendix IV for addresses.)

Royalties

It is illegal to produce copies of Ordnance Survey maps without the sanction of Her Majesty's Stationery Office.

Permission to reproduce maps for the purpose of orienteering can be obtained from the Director General, Ordnance Survey. Application is made on an appropriate form.

The first condition of obtaining permission to copy a map depends upon being able to prove that the original O.S. map is unsuitable. In the case of orienteering this is entirely true, for the map has to be corrected, altered and have additional

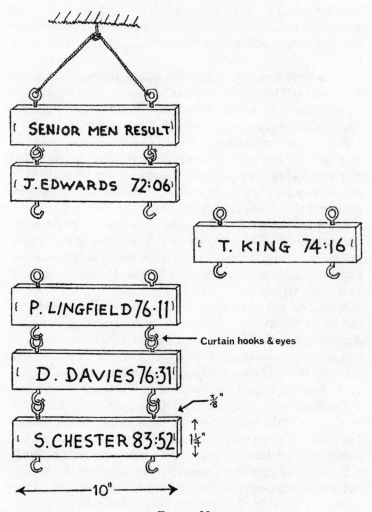

Curtain hooks & eyes

S. CHESTER 83:52

3/8"

1 1/4"

10"

FIGURE 25

A Results Ladder Board

This device, made from soft-wood board and curtain wire-hooks and eyes, makes the rapid display of results possible. It can be easily adjusted to include the position of a late result in the ranking order.

The names are written on paper which is stapled on to the boards. In a competition different coloured papers can be used to denote the various teams, so that a visual impression of a team's merit can easily be seen.

material added to it to indicate private land, out-of-bounds areas, etc., before it is suitable for competition. This situation has already been accepted by the Publication Department of the O.S.

The second condition is that the map reproductions are not being sold and being used only for business or official purposes. Orienteering races under the auspices of the various Regional Associations are acceptable to the O.S. office.

Permission to reproduce an area of Ordnance survey map can be sought for one particular reason. In this case details of the map area and number of copies, use, etc., is sent off to the O.S. at least a month before the event. The Survey then grant permission and indicate the royalty payable.

More convenient for the regular organizer of orienteering competitions is a 'Quarterly Licence'. The holder of this licence can make as many copies of maps as he wishes for orienteering purposes, and settles his account with the O.S. in retrospect at quarterly intervals.

A regional officer of an orienteering association would find this by far the most convenient way of ensuring that all reproductions printed in his area were legal. It would only be necessary for him to take stock at the end of every quarter, and calculate the total sum of royalties due from his area for each of the races in which his association was involved.

The actual cost of royalties is very reasonable and is assessed on the area of the map copied and the number of copies made. For instance, 100 copies of an area of 50 square inches, about the size of most orienteering maps, would incur a royalty of 17s 6d.

Each reproduction must bear the acknowledgement, 'Reproduced from the Ordnance Survey Map with the sanction of the Controller of H.M. Stationery Office. Crown Copyright reserved'.

The Publication Division of the O.S. are most helpful and co-operative. They will send all the regulations governing reproduction to anyone who applies for a Licence to Reproduce Ordnance Survey Maps.

9

Setting the Course

The inadvertent misplacing of one single control can completely ruin an otherwise faultless orienteering competition. A hundred hours of preparation will be wasted if something is patently wrong with the course lay-out.

The orienteer is looking forward to fair competition, firstly, between himself and the course-setter, and, secondly, between himself and fellow competitors. He does not regret travelling hundreds of miles, changing in the back of a car, and washing in a stream, if the course has been a fair challenge to his wits, skill and stamina. On the other hand, no amount of super organization, hospitality and facilities will impress him one jot, if the course was weak or unjust. Should the course actually be wrongly set, with a control misplaced either on the ground or on the master-map, then he has every right to vigorously protest and black-list the particular organization in respect of his future patronage.

It is therefore essential that course-setters take counsel from another experienced planner whenever an event is open or important. For other smaller club events, the course planner should still spend many active days, and some sleepless nights, going over the course from every angle.

The Rules of Competition (Paragraph 8) insist that in all important Open events, including championships, an outside vetting officer must be invited to check the course both on paper and physically on the ground. It is not rational to expect competitors to travel many miles to an event that has not been thoroughly inspected and approved.

ORIENTEERING

Fundamental Principles

Orienteering course-devising is as fascinating as is course-solving, and the whole exercise of matching wits against a competitive field is an intriguing balancing trick. Perhaps the hardest part of the act is to hit upon the right level of difficulty for the competitors concerned. The maxim is—keep them interested throughout, sometimes perplexed, but never discouraged. To visualize a course through the eyes of a competitor is not easy, and it is by no means a bad idea to regard the competitors as a group of 'half-blind dim-wits', who need all the help they can get to solve a course. It is an easy trap to fall into for the course-setter to over-estimate the powers of deduction of the competitor. It is far better for the orienteers to finish the race with a feeling of triumph over the course-setter than to have the situation reversed.

Although there are dozens of aspects to orienteering course-setting, several priorities need early attention, and the course-planner is well advised to bear them in mind early on in his preparations.

1. *Suitable terrain.* The type of countryside required for a race will depend to a large extent on the class of competition envisaged. Obviously, experienced performers need wild terrain to extend their qualities of skill and fitness, while at the other end of the scale, the novice is satisfied with a quite domestic area.

The initial pre-planning search for a suitable venue for a competition can start with study of the 1-in. O.S. map. Any green area bigger than 1 in. × 2 in. is worth considering; if it is surrounded by the red line of the National Trust it is a hot prospect and worth a visit. The grey dotted lines depicting common land are also encouraging clues, especially if plenty of contours are in evidence.

When a suitable geographical venue has been located, it is immediately necessary to ascertain its social availability for orienteering. The local landowners, councils, trusts, and commissions must be approached as to their attitude to competition on their property. Most landowners will respond co-operatively

110

if they are asked properly and given responsible assurance that the Country Code will be adhered to by all concerned.

Forestry Commission district officers are usually most helpful, for the Commission regards its forests as a recreative facility for the public as well as a tree-growing industry. Naturally enough, there will be areas of seedling plantations which will be out-of-bounds, and smoking and fires will be strictly forbidden.

National Trust wardens can be approached with every hope of obtaining permission to hold an event on their land, but again they will have their own laws of administration. Markers will have to be discreetly placed and no tents can be erected.

With this permission given, then the real task of setting a course begins.

2. *The Map.* The most recently revised copy of the 1 : 25,000 O.S. map should be acquired (*see* Map 1). This map should then be carefully studied at home and all the possible control sites noted, including likely points for the starts and finish of the race. This in itself is an absorbing task.

With some idea of the potential of the area the venue should be visited again. Several hours spent in travelling from likely control to control will soon establish the accuracy and completeness of the map. A map is seldom totally correct in its detail, paths change rapidly, forests are cut down and replanted, new buildings are erected and old ones decay.

The course-setter has to decide which detail is essential to the conduct of his competition, and if it is missing on the map make sure that it is added. New paths near a control site should be included, and private and out-of-bounds areas indicated.

On Forestry property in difficult terrain it may be impossible to accurately plot all the new tracks cut by the forester. In this case it is probably best to leave them all unrecorded and to ignore them as possible control sites.

3. *Selecting the problems.* An excellent method of getting the best out of the territory available is to first pick out the obvious key sections that offer a challenge to the orienteer in their solution. This technique may produce at least three excellent sections. (*See* Figure 26.) Section A–B is concerned with an over-or-round problem with a hill. Section C–D presents a

FIGURE 26
Plotting the Course

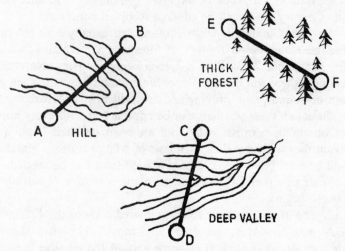

STAGE 1—Picking out the best problems.

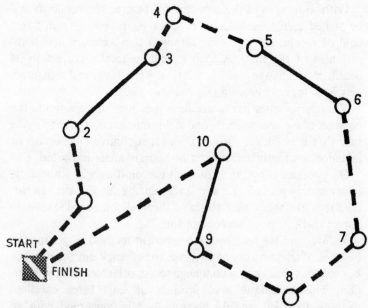

STAGE 2—Plot in the general position of other controls to produce a course of the required length.

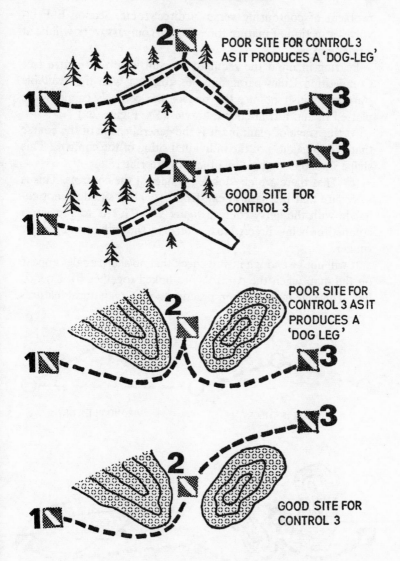

FIGURE 27
Arrangement of control positions to avoid 'dog-legs' in the course

problem of contouring versus a direct route. Section E–F involves a section of mature forest where compass work will be at a premium.

Bearing in mind the required over-all length of course (*see* Competition Rules paragraph 36), together with the available start and finish points, the rest of the controls can now be plotted in and a trial course drawn. (*See* Figure 26.)

At this stage of planning it is the general shape of the course that is important, not the individual siting of the controls. This shape should also abide by other orienteering rules:

(*a*) That there are no 'dog-leg' angles at the controls. This is to ensure that the natural exit from a control site does not coincide with the entry route. (Figure 27.) This is to prevent a competitor being directed to a control by the path of a departing runner.

It will not be enough just to check that no sharp angles appear on the map when the controls are linked together by a pencil line. This rule must work in practice too. Often natural features

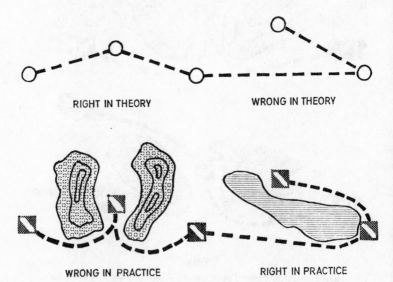

RIGHT IN THEORY   WRONG IN THEORY

WRONG IN PRACTICE   RIGHT IN PRACTICE

FIGURE 28
The 'dog-leg' in theory and in practice

will produce a dog-leg route where it does not exist on the map. (Figure 27.)

Common-sense must be applied to this situation for, as will be seen in Figure 28, a dog-leg in theory can be an obtuse angle in practice and vice versa.

(b) That wherever possible there should be a choice of routes offered between one control and the next, even if it is just a choice between equal and similar paths. (Figure 30.)

In this instance, of two similar routes around an obstacle to a control site, great care should be taken to make sure that luck and chance do not influence the outcome of the choice. If the map does not make it clear that there is a 'trap' connected with one of the alternatives, e.g. a swamp at the end of a lake, or a new thick plantation on one side of a hill, then the controls should be sited so that everyone is encouraged to go the same way. (Figure 29.)

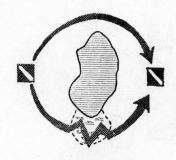

An unindicated marsh at the south end of the lake makes the choice of routes around the lake unfair.

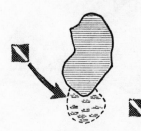

By changing the position of the second control, 'luck' is taken out of the choice. Everyone will get involved with the marsh and the subsequent detour.

FIGURE 29
Unfair Choice

ORIENTEERING

1. Acceptable choice of routes.

2. Position of controls poor, as a traverse of the cliff is encouraged.

3. Alternative position of the controls brings runners away from the danger.

FIGURE 30
Control Siting

(*c*) That the logical route between two successive controls does not encourage the competitor to traverse dangerous terrain, or to cross private property. (Figure 30.)

This rule is very important in course design.

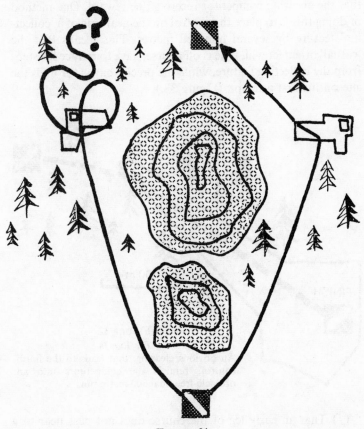

FIGURE 31

Unfair Choice

In theory either route around the hills is equal to the other. The small clearings in the forest marked on the map will give sites for direct bearings over the last few hundred yards to the control. However, if in fact the western clearing is overgrown and undetectable on the ground, then the choice is unfair. Such a situation should be avoided by the course-setter.

(*d*) That the route from the last control to the Finish naturally brings the competitors to an unobstructed run-in for the last 200 metres or so. This enables the spectators to see something of the race. (Figure 32.)

(*e*) That in experts' events the controls should be so positioned that the accurate competitor receives due reward. One method of doing this is to place the control on the near side of a 'collecting' feature by several hundred metres. This means that the 'casual' orienteer will, if he is off course, have to retrace his steps from the collecting feature, while the precise navigator finds the site on his first attempt. (Figure 33.)

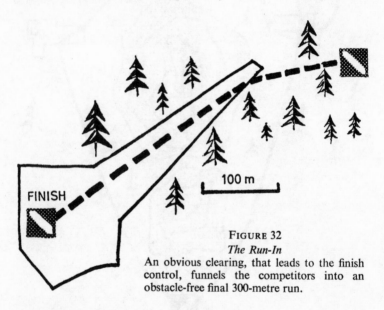

FINISH

100 m

FIGURE 32
The Run-In
An obvious clearing, that leads to the finish control, funnels the competitors into an obstacle-free final 300-metre run.

(*f*) That an early leg of the course does not pass near to a latter control. This is to prevent a lucky competitor seeing activity near a late control while in the early stages of the race, and being able to make use of this extra source of knowledge later in his circuit.

Obviously this is unfair as the early starter will not have this opportunity of gaining information.

A difficult site

An easy site

FIGURE 33

Control Sites

The position of a control in relation to a 'collecting' feature can make a section hard or easy.

(*g*) That where possible departing runners from a control do not assist 'lost' competitors. (Figure 34.)

(*h*) Finally, that there is variety in the type of problem to be solved in navigation and physical effort.

The permutating of all these desirable properties into a course of the desired difficulty and length is a complex problem for the course-setter. It will probably necessitate many hours of wandering in the forest before an acceptable route is found.

4. *The Control Site.* The actual siting of the control needs much careful thought. The Control Terminology List shows that there are at least fifty different sorts of sites for a control.

In general it is best to use features that are not only apparent on the ground but also indicated on the map. The strength of this kind of site lies in its precise indication on the map. The Rules of Competition (paragraph 17) require that the position

of controls shall be sited by reference to terrain details that can
be located with exactness by means of the map.

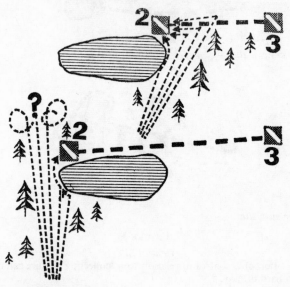

Poor—outgoing runners 'catch' and direct lost incoming runners to the control.

Good—lost runners are not
helped by outgoing runners.

FIGURE 34

Control Siting

The probable route taken away from a control should not 'catch' incoming
runners.

Such sites as 'tall tree 65 yds. S.W. of corner of wood' are
best avoided for they introduce an element of vagueness into the
proceedings.

Novices' courses will normally be best arranged with all the
controls on such sites as path junctions, bridge over stream,
trig. point, etc. All these sites are a combination between geographical features and man-made structures. On the other hand
experts will be capable of finding pure geographical features
such as knolls, ridges and re-entrants.

Whatever feature is used as a control, its description must be given with reference to the terminology listed on Maps 2 and 3. The correct use of the 'definite' and 'indefinite' article must be adopted.

5. *Positioning of the Marker Flag.* The Rules of Competition go on to ask that the actual banner marking the control be placed in strict accordance with the given written description of the control site. In practice this means that the flag must be hung on or over the designated feature. It is not acceptable for the flag to be 'just 30 yards away'. The position of the flag may shout to the hilltops to you, as the course-setter, but to the competitor, perhaps arriving from an unexpected direction, it is hidden.

In any case the competitor is probably quite willing to assume that he has made a mistake if the flag isn't patently visible at the spot he arrives at. Instead of searching behind trees or in bushes, he will circle around in an effort to re-establish his position. Only later when he has convinced himself of the rightness of his first effort will he perhaps accidentally look up in the right direction and see the flag. Orienteering is not a treasure hunt. All the marking flags should be as on the spot as possible and hanging free at head height.

The Rules, in fact, go further and suggest that should the banner be hanging next to the control site in fairly thick foliage, then the immediate area around the site should be festooned with red streamers. A site in dense undergrowth should never be used.

6. *Designation of the Control Markers.* In most events several races will be going on at the same time. The Seniors, Intermediates and Juniors will be using controls set in the same area. To avoid confusion the control markers should be labelled. For instance, the Mens' Senior fifth control would be designated S.M. 5, or a control used by the Junior Girls and the Intermediate Men could be designated J.G. 3/I.M. 7. In this case it would be the third control for the girls and the seventh control for the men.

10

The Organization of a Competition

The depth of organization of an orienteering competition will vary appreciably from events at either end of the scale of importance and size. The small Club event in a local forest involving twenty-five friends will be a simple affair compared with the championship of national size attracting hundreds of competitors. The organizer of the first kind of competition may well be the course-setter, starter and time-keeper, too. His preparation will be little more than making sure that everyone knows where to come, and at what time; his paper work confined to maps, control cards and a results sheet.

The organization of a large event will involve at least a dozen people in official capacities, and their preparations will extend through several months of planning.

But at whatever level a competition is organized, certain fundamental principles should be observed and these are based on the premise that, 'orienteering is a game of skill'.

The Rules of Competition as agreed by the British Orienteering Federation concern themselves with the most practical aspects of an event. Organizers should familiarize themselves with all these Rules and appreciate which ones are mandatory and which are permissive.

For the small 'closed' event, many of the Rules can be ignored or changed at will, for these Rules are only authoritative in the case of Open events that appear on the B.O.F.'s fixture list. A great deal of thought went into the compilation of these Rules and advice was taken from both Norway and Sweden in their framing, and in all the Committee's thinking the 'spirit' of the game was ever present.

COMPETITION RULES

Section A—General

1. *The Application of Competition Rules*

Orienteering Competitions held in Britain by Clubs affiliated to the British Orienteering Federation (B.O.F.), shall be organized in accordance with the B.O.F.'s Competition Rules. Closed Club competitions shall not necessarily be governed by all the Rules.

2. *Cross-country Orienteering*

A C.C. Orienteering race is a competition where the participants by means of map, compass and other possible navigational aids shall complete on foot the course set by the organizers in the shortest possible time. The Course is marked on a map and indicated in the terrain by certain Control Points which shall be visited in a certain sequence. The Course shall be so planned that the result depends to a large extent on the competitors' navigational skill and ability to negotiate the terrain at speed.

Some special forms of Orienteering races are dealt with under para. 3.

3. *Relay, Night, Score, Route and Line Orienteering*

(i) Relay Orienteering is a competition between teams where each individual participant runs a certain part of the Course.

(ii) Night Orienteering takes place during the hours of darkness.

(iii) Score Orienteering is a competition where the participants are given at the start a number of Controls. They shall then visit as many Controls as possible within a certain time and in any sequence. The Controls are given different points values, which shall be indicated together with their description. The result is calculated by adding up the total points collected, less a penalty of so many points per minute that the competitor is overdue at the finish.

(iv) Route Orienteering is where the competitors follow a route indicated on the ground from start to finish. Orienteering ability is tested by each competitor being required to mark exactly on his map the position of various controls passed along the route.

(v) Line Orienteering is where the competitor follows a complete course marked out on his map. Along this course Controls are placed, their position not being indicated on the map.

4. *Types of Competition*

Orienteering competitions can be described as Club, County, Regional, National or International depending upon their function.

(i) Club races are competitions where participation is limited to one or more clubs.

(ii) County, Regional and National races will be indicated on the official programme for the season.

(iii) International races are those that are listed in the International Orienteering Federation's programme.

5. *Championship Races*

(i) County and Regional Championships. Each year an annual championship should take place; if necessary the County championship can be included in the Regional race. The Regional Orienteering Association will decide in accordance with its own rules who shall arrange the championship races.

(ii) National Championships. Each year the following National Championships will take place:

Individual and Team Championship for Men

do.	Women
do.	Intermediate men
do.	do. women
do.	Junior men
do.	Junior women

and further Championships as decided by the Executive Committee of the B.O.F., who shall arrange the various National Championships.

The designated organizer of the National Championship shall, two months before the Event, send a draft invitation and programme to the B.O.F. Executive Committee for approval. Only orienteers affiliated to the B.O.F. may enter for senior or intermediate championships. The number of competitors in the various championships and each Region's quota is decided by the Executive Committee.

6. *Youth Club, School and Instructional Races*

Participation in such races as these is not conditional on membership of a Club affiliated to the B.O.F.

These races should be organized so that they are well suited for attracting new recruits to the Sport. The organizers must therefore carefully observe those rules safeguarding correct Course and correct description of Controls. The course should not be too long or difficult, and the safety of the competitors should be ensured.

Section B—Organization

7. *Notification of all Regional and other important Open Events*

The B.O.F. Executive Committee should receive notification of the dates of all Regional and other important Open Events by 15th July for the coming year—September to July.

8. *Map and Course Vetting*

At least one month before the race, the organizer of a Regional or National Championship, or of other important races, must negotiate for approval of the course with the appointed Vetting Officer. The actual course and site of the control markers will be inspected before the race, and in time for major changes to be made in the course construction and competition arrangements, if so directed by the V.O.

Vetting Officers will be appointed and assigned to these races by the Executive Committee of the B.O.F.

9. *Invitations*

Invitations to take part in Open or Championship Events should be sent at least one month before the day of competition to the Regional Associations.

The Invitation shall where possible contain the following information:

(*a*) Type of Race (Cross-country, night, score, etc.)

(*b*) Date of Race

(*c*) Classes

(*d*) Length of Course(s) by the shortest possible route.

(*e*) Type of map to be used.

(*f*) Where and when entry shall be made

(*g*) Entry fee (inc. map?)

(*h*) Time and place of venue, or alternatively, when and where this information will be available

(*i*) Team conditions

(*j*) Name of Race Organizer, and Course Planner.

If the Organizers wish to reserve the right to limit the number of competitors, the Invitation should indicate how this limitation will be made. Such reservation should be made if it seems probable that more than 200 competitors will enter.

The Invitation should also give an indication of available forms of transport to the venue area, of possible camp-sites or accommodation and whether the participant can use his own transport to report to the actual start.

10. *Private Property*

All race organizers should make sure that such areas where access is denied to the competitor are clearly indicated on the map or by warning signs. The siting of Controls that encourage a competitor to cross forbidden areas should be avoided. All necessary precautions should be taken to prevent avoidable disputes with property owners.

11. *The Race Venue*

For National and Regional Races the Organizer shall not publish the starting point before the day of the competition. For other important Open competitions the start venue can be published six days prior to the event.

At the Start, or at the Assembly area, near the Start, the following information should be displayed on a board, or given to each competitor as a hand-out:

(*a*) Name of race organizer.

(*b*) Telephone number in case of emergency.

(*c*) Time when controls will be removed,

(d) Time of closing of Finish control.

(e) For National and Regional races—a start list with start times.

(f) Further general information.

The 'warm-up' area should be clearly indicated, and competitors 'warned-off' the race area.

12. *Starting Sequence*

Competitors running the same course shall start in a sequence determined by 'seeding' or by ballot. No member of the same team shall start within 5 minutes of another member.

There should be at least 30 seconds interval between each competitor. However, for relay and other special forms of orienteering a massed start can be used.

13. *Control Card*

Each competitor shall be given a Control Card which must be carried around the Course. This will be stamped or signed at each Control. The card will be handed in at the Finish, even though the competitor fails to complete the course.

14. *The Start*

At the Start the location of the Finish should be given.

From the start the Master Map area should be clearly indicated. Should competitors be started at 1-minute or less intervals then at least 8 master maps should be available. The position of the master maps should be such that it is not possible to see the direction taken by those already started.

If master maps are displayed in the open they must be protected from the weather by a transparent cover.

15. *Indication of Controls*

On the master maps the controls shall be marked by RED circles of half a centimetre in diameter. The situation of the control shall be in the exact middle of this circle—but *not* indicated by a dot.

The control shall be described in the officially approved terminology, and may include a six-figure map reference.

The Master-map area shall be indicated by a triangle with 5 mm. sides.

The Finish shall be indicated by a double circle—5 mm. and 6 mm. in diameter with a common centre.

16. *Correction of the Map*

Every effort shall be made to indicate important omissions or differences between the map and the terrain.

17. *Location of Controls*

The Controls shall be sited by reference to terrain details that can be located with exactness by means of the map. The actual banner or flag shall be accurately placed in strict accordance to the written description.

18. *Identification of the Control*

Each Control shall be marked with an approved 'flag', which shall be coloured red and white and three-dimensional. The I.O.F. specification is for 'flags' that are prism-shaped, with each face 30 cms. square and divided diagonally with red and white colouring.

In the events where different classes are competing in the same area all controls must be designated (*see* page 121).

If a Control is located among thick foliage or for some other reason is difficult to see when arriving in its immediate vicinity, it may be desirable to festoon the immediate area around the marker with red- and white-coloured streamers.

Where a marker is easy to see on arrival in the immediate vicinity of the Control then it should be placed so that it cannot be seen from 50 yards away.

For Night Events coloured lamps or strips of fluorescent material can be used for marking the Control.

19. *The Finishing Point*

This should be indicated by a marked line. When the competitor passes over this line his time is taken to the nearest second. He then hands in his Control Card.

20. *Control Officials*

In Regional and National Events the controls should preferably be manned.

They will note the number and time of each competitor.

They will stamp or sign the competitor's control-card provided that the competitor has visited them in the nominated sequence.

The closing time of the race shall be fixed to allow the last starter ample time to complete the course. The last control shall not be removed until after this published time.

21. *Prizes*

Where possible, certificates or similar trophies should be presented on the day of competition.

Money prizes shall never be used.

22. *Details of Results*

A comprehensive result sheet should be compiled as soon as possible after the competition is over and sent to all competitors and officials.

23. *Rescue Service*

The Organizer shall ensure that a Search Party is available at the close of a competition should a competitor be missing. Where possible this party should consist of people with local knowledge.

The Organizer will also ensure that there is a supply of First Aid equipment at the Finish, together with personnel to use it. He should have the telephone number of an available local doctor.

In extremes of weather, either heat or cold, the Organizer should, if possible, provide cold or hot drinks at the Finish. He may also need to provide some cover for changing purposes, either indoors or under canvas.

Section C—The Competitor

24. *Eligibility*

All those who are affiliated to the B.O.F. either through their Club membership or through affiliation to the Regional Orienteering Association may take part in an Open or Championship Orienteering race.

The Organizers are entitled to refuse entries from those competitors who live in the immediate race area.

ORIENTEERING

25. *International Events*

A selection committee authorized by the Executive Committee shall select all British teams for International competition.

26. *Entry*

Applications to take part in an Orienteering competition should be made in writing either through the Club or by the individual competitor within the stated time and should, where it is indicated, be accompanied by the prescribed entrance fee.

The application should include the competitor's date of birth and competition class.

The Organizer may if he wishes accept late entries. He may also increase the entry fee in such cases.

Where possible late entries shall not be given the advantage of a late start-number.

27. *Dress*

The form of clothing is optional unless otherwise determined by the Organizer. In wet or cold weather clothing should provide effective protection against wind and cold.

28. *Equipment*

   (*a*) The Map. Only the map stipulated by the Organizer may be used.
   (*b*) A Protractor/Compass/Rule. A 'Silva' compass or similar instrument or instruments should be carried.
   (*c*) A watch. Should be carried by all competitors.
   (*d*) A whistle. Organizers may insist that this piece of equipment be carried in day time races in wild country. At night it should be a 'must'. The recognized International Distress Signal is six blasts on a whistle (or six shouts or flashes of a torch) at ten seconds interval for a minute, then a minute's pause, before repeating the pattern.

29. *The Country Code*

Every competitor shall show consideration towards wild life and vegetation. It is forbidden to set foot on newly-sown ground, on growing crops or on any area where the farmer has made efforts to keep animals away. Great care should be taken when crossing fences or ditches. Gates should be left as they are found.

All obvious private property is out-of-bounds.

30. *Code of Ethics*

Contests in Orienteering should be conducted in a spirit of fairness and good fellowship. Competitors must not seek to obtain unfair advantages over their fellow competitors.

Any intentional search for the position of the competition course or inspection of the area during the days preceding the race is prohibited. Violation of this rule will incur ineligibility to compete.

31. *'Hanging-on' and Collaboration*

Each competitor shall race independently. It is not allowed for a competitor to 'hang-on' to another runner. Should a competitor ignore the request of another to run independently of him, then he can be reported to the Organizer.

It is not allowed for two or more competitors to collaborate during a race, except where they are entered as a pair or a group.

32. *Abandoning the Race*

Any competitor dropping out from the race is required to report to the Organizer as soon as possible. When a contestant has reported his withdrawal to the Finish officials he is not entitled to re-enter the competition area. He should in no way assist other competitors and should avoid influencing the progress of the contest in any way.

33. *No return to Course*

Competitors who have handed in their Control Card at the Finish shall not go back on the course before the race has ended.

34. *Own Risk*

It shall be a condition of entry to an orienteering competition that the organizers shall not be liable for any damage, injury or loss suffered by a competitor however caused.

A competitor is himself responsible for any damage he may cause during the competition.

ORIENTEERING

Section D—Class Regulations

35. *Competition Classes*

Competitors in Orienteering races are divided into the following *competition classes*:

B.	Boys	under 15 years old.
G.	Girls	under 15 years old.
Jm.	Junior men	over 15 and under 18
Jw.	Junior women	over 15 and under 18
Im.	Intermediate men	over 18 and under 21
Iw.	Intermediate women	over 18 and under 21
Sm.	Senior men	21 years old and over.
Sw.	Senior women	21 years old and over.
Vm.	Veteran men	40 years old and over.
Vw.	Veteran women	40 years old and over.

Age is calculated as on the day of competition.

A Veteran can enter for a Senior event if he or she wishes.

At the discretion of the Organizer:

(*a*) An Intermediate may enter a Senior race;

(*b*) A Junior may enter an Intermediate race;

(*c*) Boys and Girls may enter a Junior race.

In the interest of safety in rough country, organizers are strongly advised to insist that Boys and Girls and Junior Women should enter as pairs or as groups.

36. *Course Distances*

The suggested normal length of the course is:

G.	..	..	1 –2 miles	(4 to 8 controls)
B.	..	..	1½–2½ miles	(5 to 9 controls)
Jw.	..	..	1½–2½ miles	(5 to 9 controls)
Jm.	..	..	2½–3 miles	(5 to 9 controls)
Iw.	..	..	2½–3 miles	(5 to 9 controls)
Im.	..	..	3 –3½ miles	(6 to 9 controls)
Sw.	..	..	3 –3½ miles	(6 to 9 controls)
Sm. (Standard)		4 – miles	(7 to 10 controls)
Sm. (Elite)	..	5½–8 miles	(9 to 14 controls)
Novices..	..	3 –3½ miles	(6 to 9 controls)

These distances refer to best possible routes, and not to straight-line measurements.

(Special rules apply to Night Events—*see* Section 37.)

ORIENTEERING

Section E—Various Special Rules

37. *Night Orienteering*

Orienteering races at night can be held as Individual Competitions for Intermediates, Seniors and Veteran Classes. Boys and Girls and Junior Women must compete as pairs or groups and will accompany each other throughout the race.

At the discretion of the Organizer, Junior Men may compete as individuals.

Each competitor shall carry a whistle.

The Course should be planned so that competitors shall not have to negotiate precipitous or otherwise dangerous terrain.

The Controls can be marked by the normal 'flags', coloured lamps or light reflectors.

Senior courses should seldom exceed $3\frac{1}{2}$ miles.

38. *Relay Orienteering*

A competitor is only allowed to run one stage. Participants on the same team must be members of the same Club.

39. *Team Events*

Senior men .. .. up to 8 nominated—5 to count.
All other classes .. up to 5 nominated—3 to count.

Groups and pairs have their own competition within the appropriate class.

Up to five pairs nominated—three to count.

Normally the competitor's time is used in the determination of a Team result, not his position in the race.

Section F—Protests

40. *Protest against a Competitor*

Competitors and accredited officials may protest to the Race Organizer against a competitor who is thought to have contravened the B.O.F.'s Competition Rules or the special regulations that apply to the race in question. The protest shall be in writing and handed in as soon as possible after the Finish and at the latest the same day.

The Organizer shall give a decision on the protest, which shall either acquit, warn or exclude the competitor from being placed.

Even without a protest, the Organizer can exclude a competitor from being placed, should he have contravened the competition rules.

The decision shall be communicated to the parties in writing, informing them that an appeal can be made to the Regional Association with 14 days.

41. *Protest against the Arrangements*

Competitors and officials may protest to the Regional Association if it is thought that the Organizer has held a race that contravened the B.O.F.s Competition Rules.

The protest should be received in writing within 48 hours of the race, and should include a fee of 5s., which will be refunded if the protest is upheld.

The Rules of Competition apply not only to the conduct of the race itself but also to many of the necessary 'official' arrangements. Some of these rules are concerned with the programming of the administration and organizers will need to employ a timetable of activity for their events.

'... *advice should neither be given nor sought*'

Organizing an Orienteering Event . . . Check List

A. *For a cross-country Championship Event or large Open Race*

When to do	*What to do*
By July 15th of the year	Inform the B.O.F. Executive of the Event, date and area.
4 months ahead	1. The Organizing Committee formed. 2. The Regional Associations and Clubs informed of the general arrangements, classes, etc. 3. Venue selected with reference to suitable *and* available terrain and facilities. 4. Production of Entry forms, etc. 5. Trophies ordered.
6 weeks ahead	1. Course planned. 2. Details of event with entry forms distributed. 3. Officials designated tasks. 4. First Aid and Rescue arrangements made. 5. Police and Press informed.
4 weeks ahead	1. Course inspected by Vetting Officer. 2. Maps reproduced or ordered.
2 weeks ahead	1. Last entries accepted. 2. Start List compiled by ballot. 3. Check transport, catering and spectator arrangements. 4. Control cards produced (see below—i). 5. Recorder's Sheets produced (see below—ii). 6. Route Cards produced (see below—iii). 7. Instructions to competitors produced (see below—iv).
6 days ahead	1. Rendezvous published. 2. Further information to the Press. 3. Master-Maps produced.
Day of Event	1. Control flags in position, and checked by V.O. 2. Rendezvous, start, control and finish officials briefed and placed. 3. First Aid and Rescue arrangements confirmed. 4. Results compiled and announced. 5. Prize giving. 6. Site cleared.
After the competition	1. Results sent to all competitors and officials. 2. Letters of thanks to all who donated facilities and services to the event.

B. *For an Inter-Club Score Event*

When to do	*What to do*
6 weeks ahead	Advise Club secretaries of date, type and general venue of the event.
4 weeks ahead	Suitable terrain found, inspected and permission sought for use.
2 weeks ahead	1. Control points settled. 2. Starting Point arranged. 3. Maps reproduced (see Map 11). 4. Control sheets produced (see below—v).
6 days ahead	Venue announced to Club secretaries.
Day of event	1. All control markers in position. 2. Officials briefed and positioned. 3. Results compiled and announced. 4. Tidy up site.
After the event	1. Results and comments sent out to all competitors, together with details of next events. 2. Thank-you letters where necessary.

(i) *Example of Control Card for a Cross-country Event*

Hrs. Mins. Secs.

Start No. ....   Finish Time ....

Class ....   Start Time ....

Club/School ....   Time Taken ....

Name ....   Place ....

1	2	3	4	5	6
7	8	9	10	11	12

(ii) *An example of a Recorder's Sheet for Cross-country Events*

RECORDER'S SHEET

Start No./Time	Name	Class	Team	Finish Time	Time Taken	Controls Missed	Position

CLASSES   REMARKS

B.	Boys
G.	Girls
Jm.	Junior men
Jw.	Junior women
Im.	Intermediate men
Iw.	Intermediate women
Sm.	Senior men
Sw.	Senior women
Vm.	Veteran men
Vw.	Veteran women

ORIENTEERING

(iii) *An example of a Control Description sheet—Route Card*

The Blankshire County Championships

SENIOR MEN

PLEASE NOTE

ROUTE CARD

1.	766 389	The stream source
2.	787 393	The hill summit
3.	791 403	The neck
4.	773 408	A stile on the path
5.	783 419	The clearing
6.	796 421	The easternmost knoll
7.	806 407	A ruin on the stream
8.	795 418	The wood west point
9.	814 411	The depression
Finish	816 408	The Farm building

In EMERGENCY ring
*OAL*523465
Controls 8 & 9 will be
removed at 4.00 p.m.

Traverse of areas marked
'Out of Bounds' will
mean disqualification

(iv) *Instructions to Competitors*

This sheet will contain important information that the organizer wishes to bring to the notice of every competitor.

As much of this information will concern SAFETY and the welfare of the competitor, sufficient time must be given for its reading and understanding. It should be handed to each competitor at the same time as he reports his arrival, and this should be at least 30 minutes before his starting-time.

It will generally contain:

(*a*) A description of the out-of-bounds areas, e.g. those areas coloured blue on the map, or that are inside a solid black line.

(*b*) A notice of hazards—cliffs, swamps and deep rivers, and instructions as to their crossing, e.g. The River Wey should only be crossed by the available bridges.

(*c*) A designation of a 'safety-handrail', so that in the event of a competitor becoming completely lost he can be told to travel in a certain direction to regain civilization. E.g. Walk due north until the A 5432 is reached—this road will be 'swept' at 5.30 p.m.

(*d*) The closing-out times of the last few controls and the

Finish. E.g. Controls 8 and 9 will be removed at 4.00 p.m. and the Finish closed at 4.30 p.m.

(e) All competitors, whether they complete the course or not, MUST report in person (or by telephone in an emergency) to the Finish.

(f) A note explaining accident procedure. E.g. If a competitor finds a casualty he should take the following action: (i) In a severe case, where the injured should obviously be kept company, abandon the race—remember this is only a game. Make the patient as comfortable as possible, keep him warm. Give the distress signal—whistle or shout six times a minute every alternate minute. If no help comes mark the map accurately for your position and make for the nearest control that you believe to be manned.
(ii) In the event of finding a sprained ankle case, etc., mark the position of the accident and continue to the next control and report the facts.

(v) *An example of a Control Sheet for a SCORE Event*

CONTROL CHECK SHEET

SOUTHERN NAVIGATOR'S CLUB—SCORE EVENT— HOLMWOOD

NAMES..(Please use BLOCK letters)

TEAM.. CLASS..

NUMBER		Hours	Minutes	Seconds		
	FINISH TIME				SCORE	
	START TIME				PENALTY	
	TIME LATE			TOTAL		
	PENALTY			PLACE		

(continued overleaf)

ORIENTEERING

Control Number	Map Ref.	Description	Points Value	Control Stamp
1	137 464	The Trig. Point	45	
2	160 458	The stream source	25	
3	155 457	The well	15	
4	142 454	The pond	35	
5	147 454	The track and the path junct.	20	
6	158 454	The Trig. Point	10	
7	151 451	The wood east point	15	
8	144 447	The track end	20	
9	160 445	The stream source	10	
10	157 444	The well	10	
11	142 443	The pulpit	35	
12	140 438	The stream junction	35	
13	144 438	The hill summit	30	
14	153 440	The Hill Fort	10	
15	139 433	The spring	40	
16	139 426	The niche	45	
17	155 423	The lake southernmost point	40	

N.B. 1. The TOTAL TIME ALLOWED is 90 mins.
2. The PENALTY RATE is 1 point for 6 seconds.

(*See between* pages 48–9.)

ORIENTEERING

The Start Area

The mechanics of organizing a large championship are very complex. A great deal of the extra complexity—extra that is over the small inter-club event—is made by the necessity of keeping the site of the competition secret until the day of the event.

This involves the organizers in the problem of transport from a rendezvous point or an assembly area to the actual starting point. Also if the start and finish points are separate, there is the transport of competitors or their baggage to consider.

The easiest solution to the problem is to have an 'out-and-back' course commencing and finishing at the assembly area, with a rendezvous site previously announced. (*See* Figure 35.)

The Rendezvous

Where there is accommodation for changing and washing at the Start, the rendezvous point can be at a convenient centre for public transport, such as a railway station car park. Here instructions will be given to competitors with cars on how to proceed to the Assembly area, and hired transport will carry those who have arrived at the rendezvous by public transport. An indication can be given, when the position of the rendezvous is announced, of the time needed to travel from the rendezvous to the assembly area.

The Assembly Area

It is in this area that the competitors report, receive further information, their instructions, and confirmation of their starting-times.

They will also prepare for the competition—changing, etc.

If there has been a rendezvous separate from the assembly area, then competitors will proceed on foot to the actual starting position. However, if the assembly area was also the previously announced rendezvous, then the competitors will be transported by bus to the actual start.

The Starting Point

This is best divided into a 'Calling-up Station' and the actual 'Start and Master-map Point'.

ORIENTEERING

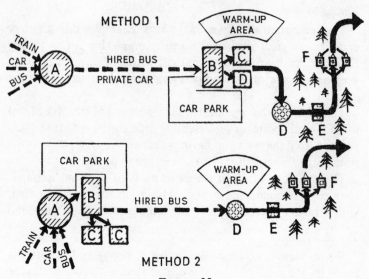

FIGURE 35

Starting arrangements

A — Rendezvous.
B — Assembly area.
C — Changing facilities.
D — Calling-up area.
E — Start.
F — Master-maps.

Competitors should be 'called' ten to twenty minutes before their individual start time and their details checked.

Calling-up Station

Here the following procedure can take place:
 (i) Name, class, etc., checked.
 (ii) Numbers given to competitors.
 (iii) Maps given to competitors.
 (iv) Control Card given to competitors.
 (v) Competitors sent off to the Start—i.e. to follow coloured streamers to the Start.

Start

This can be several minutes' walk away from the calling-up

142

area. The time element should be such that the competitors have at least five minutes to wait after arrival at the Start.

At the Start

(i) Competitor checks his map and is told of any hazards, etc., not indicated on the map.

(ii) One minute before his start-time, he is given his Control Description Sheet and allowed to pass through a barrier—i.e. a simple rope between trees.

(iii) At his start-time, best indicated by a whistle-blast (this helps to tick-off time for those waiting), he is set-off for the master maps. Again he can be asked to follow streamers but the distance from Start to Master Maps should be short—under 100 metres if possible.

Start Times (Alternative for Club races)

In large events, other than championship competitions, the problem of human mechanics in connection with start-times is a vexed one. Too often the good work that goes into the compilation of a Starting List goes for nothing, because of delays and absences at the actual start. Not only do competitors arrive late, after their advertised start-time, but extra runners expect to be included at the last moment. Consequently a more flexible method of allocating start-times is desirable.

An excellent method is for the organizer to allocate a starting period to each competitor, and ask about ten entries to report in each 15-minute period. The competitor then reports at the assembly area, changes and is then directed to the starting area. The steward in charge of this operation channels runners to the starter at regular intervals.

The starter then gives the competitor his exact starting time at the moment he sends him to the master-map area. This method does away with all the confusion and ambiguities of altered start-times, but still ensures a regular supply and flow of competitors going to the start.

Master-Map Area

This area will be close to the Start—20 to 100 yards away and if possible out of sight of the Start area.

ORIENTEERING

There should be at least eight master-maps available for use for every class, and they should be covered with clear plastic to protect them from the weather. They can be mounted on card stuck on drawing boards or hung on fences and trees.

In Score Events multiple starts are permissible and as many competitors can be started at one time as there are master-maps available.

The gathering of information from the master-map is a vital part of the race and careful consideration should be given by the organizer to the site and presentation of the maps.

One good arrangement is to mount the master-maps on a flat surface—a plank of wood, a fence or a table, and to leave room at the side of each map for the competitor to rest his map also on a flat smooth surface. For a night event a door laid on the ground with a Tilley lamp hung over it makes an excellent surface for the competitors to kneel around and do their copying.

The Control Sites

In all large and important events officials should man the controls. Firstly, to make sure that the 'flag' is not removed, and secondly, to ensure that all the competitors circulate around the course in the specified manner. The Rules of Competition ask that a competitor's Control Card should only be stamped if the previous 'boxes' have been correctly marked.

Officials at the controls can also take the times of the competitors as they pass through, as this information will be of interest to the organizer when he makes up his report of the event. It will, for instance, indicate which runners did best over various sections of the course.

Several controls at key sections of the course should, if possible, be in radio contact with the Finish, so that the progress of various competitors can be passed on to spectators and officials. Radio contact will also provide an extra safety facility.

The Finish

The Rules ask that the run-in to a marked finishing line be un-interrupted. This will give the spectators a chance of seeing some real activity and will enable the competitors to have a final physical fling over the last 200 or 300 metres.

ORIENTEERING

A timekeeper and recorder will take the finishing time and the name and number of the competitor. The Control Card will also be collected as it will be needed to check that all the controls have been visited.

If the Finishing Area is not within walking distance of the Start or Assembly Area, then arrangements will have to be made for either the transport of baggage to the Finish or transport of the competitor back to his warm clothes and refreshments, etc.

Added interest is given to the finish arrangements if an indication of finishing order can be displayed. A large board, either a blackboard or a specially designed panel, can be kept up to date with not only the final times of the runners but also, if the information is available, their times at various stages of the race. (*See* Figure 25.)

'. . . *control* 10 *will be removed at* 4 *p.m.*'

11

Fitness Training for Orienteering

Most of us enjoy being reasonably successful at the game of our choice and we hope and expect to improve steadily, if only to the extent of being next to last rather than last.

Personal improvement in orienteering can come from two sources, first from an increase in the skills of navigation, and secondly from an increase in fitness and running ability.

The art of wayfinding is developed by intelligent application of methods and techniques explained in earlier chapters of this book. Regular practice will groove these 'tricks of the trade' into a reliable pattern of procedure, and each successful decision made in the forest will strengthen the learning process. We not only learn by doing, but also remember best that which gave us the most satisfaction.

The other half of the formula for success is the ability to move fast and continuously for over an hour in rough terrain. The word 'fast' is a relative one for all of us. For some of us it will just mean jogging, rather than walking, on all the flat sections of the course; while to the younger and more ambitious orienteer 'fast' movement is synonymous with rapid running on the level and quick jogging uphill.

Actually, running is a very simple activity and the technique of moving from place to place on two legs is easily learnt. As long as it is appreciated that the left leg is not used twice in succession then there isn't much more to learn and most of us are reasonably efficient in this skill. The difference between Ron Clark, world record holder for 3 miles on the track, and Fred Bloggs, occasional finisher in orienteering events, is not so much in the running action of the two men but in the number of hours that each of them trains a week. It is an indisputable fact in running that success on the track is in a direct ratio to the number of miles covered in training.

The average orienteer is not perhaps concerned with producing a sub-13-minute three-miles on the track, but he is likely to want to raise a gallop on all the runnable sections of the course during a 100-minute race. Running training will help him achieve this degree of fitness and directly increase his enjoyment factor in orienteering events.

Daily training for 1 hour will produce wonderful results, particularly if the 60 minutes are full of activity and do not include the fringe activities of getting changed, having a chat to training colleagues, showering and dressing afterwards. Serious orienteers will find little hardship in devoting an hour a day to their training, and with this level of fitness they will probably compete in occasional athletic or cross-country races too. Their work-outs will be much the same as those done by 3- and 6-milers and their attitude to schedules and weekly mileage much the same.

However, many orienteers are likely to subscribe to a less intensive régime of training and only be prepared to spend three days a week on training. A modest 30 minutes every other day will produce excellent general fitness and allow a high degree of functional vigour to be attained.

This 90 minutes a week training investment will be far more effective if it is set in a general pattern of physical awareness. The orienteer who goes out of his way to do physical work throughout the day can quickly raise his general level of fitness and supplement his training sessions. If he never rides when he can walk, never walks when he can trot, never uses the lift when there are stairs—he can soon pack quite a lot of incidental training into every twenty-four hours. A competitive attitude to life can also help a fitness programme. No one should ever be able to overtake a man with training on his mind, whether it be on foot, on a bicycle or when climbing steps. The next corner should be reached before that fellow commuter twenty yards ahead. Every dance should be danced, every girl's suitcase carried (unless she happens to be the orienteer), every stalled car pushed. If the eyes are kept open there are dozens of opportunities every day for the man in training to add to his sum total of exercise. Take every opportunity to move, carry and climb and strength must grow.

Basic Running Training

STAGE I. Three sessions a week of jogging. Start with 10 minutes (about a mile). Add each day a further 2 to 3 minutes of jogging until 30 minutes is reached. Stay at 30 minutes jogging but increase the speed of the jog until it becomes a run and can be kept up for the full 30 minutes.

All this work should be done dressed in warm clothes, with rubber shoes on the feet, and take place in the local park or grass verge of the road.

STAGE 2. (*To be started when Stage 1 becomes routine*). After 10 minutes jogging and quiet running to warm-up, a number of different forms of running training can be done. These workouts are described below and can be done in rotation throughout the week. None of them need any special facility for their attainment, but two things should be remembered about running training. Firstly, it is a fairly boring activity. This boredom can be countered by training in company, perhaps at the local athletic track, or by running in different surroundings as often as possible. Secondly, that the discipline of training for running is an internal one and that each man must come to terms with his own laziness or otherwise. Again, running with others will generally produce a better result and certainly help the miles along.

(*a*) *Interval Running*. This particular form of exercise was developed by Emil Zatopek, the great Czech middle-distance runner, and brought to a climax by Britain's Gordon Pirie. It consists of fast and slow periods of running. For instance, should the interval be 200 metres, then the man runs hard for this distance and then rests for a couple of minutes before repeating the dose. The interval can vary from 150 to 250 metres, and the hardness of the work-out can be increased by three methods:

ORIENTEERING

(i) Running the fast piece faster.

(ii) Reducing the period of recovery.

(iii) Increasing the number done.

This method of training increases the heart-volume and develops the capillarization of the musculature, and if done regularly will give a better return for effort than any other form of training. Three factors should be taken into consideration and must be favourably attuned to one another:

(i) Duration of effort—this should be relatively short and not longer than 40 seconds.

(ii) Intensity of effort—this should be strong but not fierce, approximately 80 per cent of the runner's maximum performance.

(iii) Duration of recovery period—this should be reduced from about 2 minutes to no less than 30 seconds.

In practice a work-out would be as follows:

The orienteer can run 200 metres flat-out in 30 seconds; therefore his training rate should be 20 per cent slower, i.e. about 36 seconds. The number of times he can attain this effort in a work-out will depend on the man's condition, but usually it will be between 6–20 times, and will, of course, increase as the training takes its effect over the weeks. The interval for recovery again will vary from 2 minutes down to about 75 seconds as the training develops. This period of recovery should be connected with the ability of the heart and breathing to become calm again. As soon as a feeling of freshness is regained the hard work should be repeated.

(b) *Continuous Running.* The weakness of interval running training is its great monotony whether it is done on the athletic track or at the side of the road. It also fails to condition the mind to accepting long periods of continuous activity.

For these two reasons most runners resort to 'free' running in the fields and woods, and devise a course of 3 to 6 miles which they can run round and receive the stimulation of spiritual release from the monotony of training up and down in the one place.

These work-outs should be done on a good surface where possible and be timed. Other factors such as slope and prevailing

ORIENTEERING

wind should also be in the runner's favour. An ideal course would be one that descended several hundred feet over four or so miles with the wind normally blowing on the athlete's back. The start could be reached by jogging for 20 to 30 minutes along the diameter of the semi-circular course.

These longer runs will promote general organic stamina and also condition the mind.

Most fatigue is 'all in the mind', and often although our brain tells us that we are too tired to go on, the body is still nowhere near its breaking point. During these long continuous runs the orienteer will be subjected to all the mental visions of collapse that are associated with continuous effort. Over the weeks he will learn to fight his way through these 'black-periods' and accept the fact that it is always possible to keep going a little bit further.

External stimuli often push fatigue to the back of the mind. The sight of a possibly pretty girl on a bike ahead, or the recognition of friends passing in a car, often enable another mile to be covered, even after you have already made up your mind to pack it in at the next telegraph-pole. Experiences like these enforce the ability to keep trying, and the recognition that nothing is as bad as it first seems.

(c) *Fartlek*. Is a Swedish word which means 'speed-play', and was popularized by the great Swedish athletes of 1930's under the national coach Gösta Holmer. It is a combination of quantities of easy running, interspersed with fast sprints, strides,

FIGURE 36
Fartlek Running Training

and periods of uphill resistance running. It is done in pleasant surroundings, in woods, parklands or golf courses and a normal work-out might last for 60 minutes.

It would be wrong to lay down a set pattern for Fartlek training, but the following kinds of running should appear several times during the work-out.

   (i) Fast 75 yards sprints on a level surface.

  (ii) Steady strides (at about 70–75 seconds for the quarter-mile speed) for 800–1,000 metres.

 (iii) Uphill rushes for 50–100 metres.

 (iv) Jogging for 6 minutes with fast 15-metre bursts of speed thrown in every half minute or so.

  (v) Down the slope runs, trying to keep the legs driving although the speed increases, for 200 metres.

Fartlek training when done properly is tough, demanding and most effective—it should not be allowed to degenerate into an indiscriminate jogging session.

(*d*) *Terrain Negotiation*. The problems of fast continuous movement in orienteering races are multiplied by the variety of surfaces that the countryside presents. The going can vary between the tarmac of a road to the vertical jungle of an uncleared elder grove.

The technique of covering bracken slopes at speed remains undiscovered, but practice over other unsympathetic surfaces does produce results. In general, smaller steps, especially uphill, tend to keep a rhythm going and help retain some vestige of running form. Smaller steps also tend to throw less strain on the landing leg should the ground be pit-falled or rocky.

However, strength in the ankles and confidence to leap from tussock to tussock will vary from orienteer to orienteer. The experienced fell-runner will soon pass the trained athlete on the downhill section of a race. The athlete is still trying to run downhill, while the fell runner is allowing his body to be dragged by gravity and is just sticking out a leg now and then to prevent his body hitting the ground. At the moment of crisis he lands with both feet together like a parachute jumper and expects and allows the surface of rubble or scree to carry him forward.

ORIENTEERING

If possible, sections of the Fartlek training should include negotiation of rough terrain. The path should be abandoned and heather, gorse, scree and fallen trees should be tackled. In all this work the vital factor is to keep up your forward momentum. Mechanically speaking, starting from still is many times more energy-consuming than is continued motion; consequently, locomotion should be steady. Very steep slopes should be taken by a series of tacks backwards and forwards across the plane of the slope, and boggy ground crossed with small steps rather than tremendous jumps. Plenty of practice will solve most of the problems of rough terrain traversing and will in itself be an excellent form of resistance-running training.

A Training Diary

This should be a continuous and comprehensive record of all training work-outs and competitive events of your career. Its value lies mainly in the future. Fitness and running training is a logical progression not only from week to week but also from year to year. There is little doubt you can remember what happened in training last week, but you soon want to know what you were doing in training last month or this time last year. By analysing the work done, and being reminded of mistakes made in the past, it is possible to decide what sort of training is necessary for success in the future.

The daily or thrice weekly write-up of work need not be long, in fact it can be reduced to a few lines if some form of shorthand or speed-writing is devised. The record should include items such as the venue of the work-out, the weather, the company, results and personal impressions. The following lay-out could be adopted with advantage:

The hardest part of any training programme is not the actual physical business of running but the overcoming of the mental inertia in all of us. Once the effort has been made and you are outside your front door, dressed and ready for action, the main difficulty of the training session is over.

Get into the habit of going training at a certain time and the battle of personal fitness is half won. Regular training will not only help you enjoy your orienteering race more than ever, but

ORIENTEERING

Page from a Training Diary
 (A loose-leaf book.)

Date: Wed. 13th April 1966. 6.0 p.m.
Weather: Cool with wind.
Venue: The Harriers Track—in good shape.
Work: Warmed-up 10 mins.
8 × 200 metres in 33 secs. . . . last one 34·6.
(recovery period of 90 secs.)
O All running done in warm-up shoes. Eight seem to be getting easier. Trained for 45 mins.

Date: Friday, 15th April 1966. 7.30 p.m.
Weather: Wet.
Venue: Jessop's Woods and Common.
Work: Did Fartlek session. Six sprints up White Hill. Four circuits of King's Mere—best time 2 : 18·7 secs. Jogged on road side for 15 minutes at end of workout. Trained for 55 mins.

Date: Sunday, 17th April 1966. 10.45 a.m.
Weather: Fine.
Venue: Heathside, Fordham.
Work: The Mole Orienteering Club Open Event.
17th in 102 mins. 17·5 secs.
Made a stupid mistake at Control 1 (again) overshot
O the marker and spent 10 minutes looking in the wrong valley. Resolve to walk to No. 1 next time! After that went well, except for No. 6, which seemed to baffle everyone who tried to cross the neck of forest direct. Also marked circle for No. 7 about 50 metres wrong—mistakes like this make it worth while going over the master-maps twice just to check. Do this next time.
The Club finished 3rd. Gerry was 7th for our best result.

---

will also pay a dividend on your attitude to life in general. A larger appetite for living and a smaller waist-line will be two of the more obvious bonuses.

'. . . most fatigue is in the mind.'

12

'The Last Word'

The adventure of orienteering is there for you to find. Like most other things in this life the more you put in the more you'll get out. As you will have gathered, there is a great deal to learn in this sport and a lifetime to do it. Take a pride in doing things the right way and become a craftsman in the game.

At the top level of the sport, competition is fiercely competitive and several years of training in both technique and fitness will need to be devoted to the game before consistent success is achieved. Great performers in sport, and orienteering is no exception, are planted in the winter, cultivated in the spring and bloom in the summer. The size and perfection of the flower will increase each year as the roots dig down each winter and the plant becomes strong and mature.

At a lower level of functional vigour the sport offers rewards to the participant which are both physical and spiritual. Orienteering is recreative in the original sense of the word. During the challenge of each event the individual has his 'batteries' recharged and a feeling of release from the mechanics of life is experienced.

This is a complete sport, the body is exercised and the mind is absorbed—the criterion of success is your personal enjoyment.

May you gain as many glorious memories from the sport as I have done in the past, and intend to do in the future.

British Orienteering Federation Constitution

1. TITLE AND PURPOSE

The Federation shall be called 'British Orienteering Federation'. The objects of the Federation shall be to encourage, promote and control the Sport of Orienteering in the United Kingdom.

2. MANAGEMENT

(*a*) The affairs of the Federation shall be conducted by an Executive Committee which shall consist of a Chairman, a Secretary, a Treasurer and two representatives of each constituent Association. In addition the senior executive officer of the Scottish Orienteering Association who does not hold office in the Federation shall, *ex officio*, be a member of the Executive Committee. The Executive Committee shall meet and act as required for the efficient conduct of the Federation's business but in any event not less than once per year. An appropriate officer shall maintain a Minute Book and record in it the business of all Meetings and the names of those present. A Quorum shall consist of not less than one-third of the total strength of the Committee.

(*b*) The officers of the Federation, to be elected annually at the Annual General Meeting, shall consist of the Chairman, Secretary and Treasurer of the Executive Committee. To these officers may be added a President. If any vacancy should occur amongst the officers, the Executive Committee shall have power to fill the post until the next Annual General Meeting. The Chairman shall not serve as such for more than three years consecutively.

(c) The Executive Committee shall have power to:

    (1) Appoint additional officers but if these come from outside the Committee they shall not have a vote.

    (2) Constitute sub-committees as may be deemed necessary.

    (3) Co-opt up to four extra members but these members shall not have a vote.

(d) One of the two Executive Committee representatives from each Constituent Association must have finished in three Open Competitions (recognized by the B.O.F.) in the two years prior to his nomination.

3. CONSTITUENT ASSOCIATIONS

(a) The Constituent Associations entitled to be represented on the Executive Committee are:

    The Scottish Orienteering Association.

    The Northern Ireland Orienteering Association.

    The Welsh Orienteering Association.

    Each of the Area Associations of England whose territories shall coincide with those of the Regional Sports Councils.

(b) Adjustments may be made to these boundaries if so approved by the Executive Committee and submitted to the next General Meeting for approval.

(c) Each Constituent Association must submit its Constitution for approval by the Executive Committee before its representatives are entitled to vote. Any amendments that may be made from time to time must also be approved by the Executive Committee. If approval is withheld, two representatives of the excluded Association may appeal to the next General Meeting.

4. MEMBERSHIP

Membership fees shall be fixed for the ensuing year at the Annual Meeting.

Members of the British Orienteering Federation are defined thus:

(a) *Individuals*

Senior and Intermediate men and women who are members

of their Area Association and who have paid their membership fee through their Area Association.

(*b*) *Clubs*

Clubs which are affiliated to their Area Association and which have paid their membership fees for each senior (and intermediate) man and woman. These fees must be paid through the Area Associations.

(*c*) *Non-Specialist Groups*

Groups or Organizations which cover a number of activities (Y.M.C.A.s, County Associations of Youth Clubs, etc.) and whose members only take part in Orienteering competitions on an occasional basis (i.e. no member takes part in more than two Open Competitions per year) and which have paid their membership fees through their Area Associations.

(*d*) *Youth Clubs and Schools*

Youth Clubs and Schools, all of whose members (except the leaders) are below the age of 21 and which have paid their membership fee through their Area Associations. No Youth Club or School shall have more than three leaders over the age of 21.

(*e*) *Corporate Membership*

National Organizations (National Association of Youth Clubs, National Association of Boys Clubs, Boy Scouts, Girl Guides, etc.) which have paid their membership fee direct to the British Orienteering Federation.

(*f*) *Honorary Life Membership*

This shall be accorded to persons who have given outstanding service to Orienteering and have been recommended by the Executive Committee and their nomination approved at the Annual General Meeting.

Special Note

If there is no Area Association then Individuals, Clubs, Non-Specialist Groups, Youth Clubs and Schools in that Area may affiliate to the British Orienteering Federation on application to the Executive Committee.

5. VOTING

All members of the Federation have the right to vote at the General Meeting. The voting shall be as follows:

(*a*) Individuals: one vote.

(*b*) Each paid-up senior and intermediate Club member present at the meeting shall have one vote.

(*c*) Clubs: A duly authorized official of the Club will have one vote for each paid-up senior and intermediate man or woman in that club not at the Meeting.

(*d*) Non-Specialist Groups: one vote.

(*e*) Youth Clubs and Schools: one vote.

(*f*) Corporate Members: one vote.

No proxy votes allowed.

6. FINANCE

(*a*) The Financial Year of the Federation shall run from 1st April to 31st March each year. The accounts of the Federation will be balanced at 31st March each year and submitted, after independent audit, to the Annual General Meeting that follows the audit.

(*b*) All cheques written against Federation funds shall be signed by the Treasurer and one officer as defined in Clause 2(b).

(*c*) The Federation shall have the power to fix a levy on all entry fees for Open Events. The amount of the levy shall be decided by the Executive Committee by a two-thirds majority of the whole Committee and its continuance shall be subject to approval at the next Annual General Meeting.

7. RULES OF COMPETITION AND BYE-LAWS

The Executive Committee shall be empowered to publish and enforce such Rules of Competition and Bye-laws as they feel will be beneficial to the affairs of the Federation. Two-thirds of the entire Executive Committee must approve the rules of competition and any bye-laws before they become operative.

8. PARTICIPATION IN CHAMPIONSHIPS

All competitors aged 21 and over at Regional and National Championships shall be members of the B.O.F. as defined in Clauses 4(a) and 4(b) of this Constitution.

9. ANNUAL GENERAL MEETING

The Federation should hold an Annual General Meeting between 1st April and 30th June each year. If possible this meeting should be held on the same week-end and in the same Area as the British National Championships.

10. EXTRAORDINARY GENERAL MEETING

An Extraordinary General Meeting may be called by the Executive Committee or on an application in writing to the Secretary which is supported by 10 per cent of the total voting membership of the Federation.

11. NOTICES

(a) Any amendment to the Constitution shall be proposed in writing to the Secretary at least one calendar month before the Annual General Meeting or any Extraordinary Meeting.

(b) The Agenda of the Annual General Meeting and of any Extraordinary General Meeting shall be sent to all members not less than fourteen days before the meeting.

12. ALTERATIONS TO THE CONSTITUTION

Alterations to the Constitution require a simple majority at the Annual General Meeting or any Extraordinary General Meeting that may be called under Clause 10.

List of names and addresses of Secretaries of the Regional Associations of the United Kingdom

1. The British Orienteering Federation: Mr. Gerry Charnley, 2 Stanley Villas, Hoghton, Preston, Lancs.
2. The Scottish Orienteering Association: Mr. H. R. Philip, 47 Corslet Road, Currie, Midlothian.
3. The East Midlands Orienteering Association (Derbyshire, Notts., Leics., Lincolns., Northants, Rutland): Mr. N. A. Taylor, 6 Gregory Boulevard, Nottingham.
4. The West Midlands Orienteering Association (Hereford, Salop, Stafford, Worcs., Warwicks.): Mr. M. Griffin, 1 Park Head Road, Dudley, Worcestershire.
5. The North West Orienteering Association (Lancs., Cheshire, Cumberland, Westmorland): Mr. Gerry Charnley, 2 Stanley Villas, Hoghton, Preston, Lancs.
6. The Southern Orienteering Association (Hants., Berks., Bucks., Oxon., I. of W.): Mr. Keith Parris, 'Walden', Emery Down, Lyndhurst, Hants.
7. The South West Orienteering Association (Cornwall, Devon, Dorset, Somerset, Wilts., Glos.): Mr. E. Peckett, 36 Higher Holcombe Road, Teignmouth, Devon.
8. The South-East Orienteering Association (Surrey, Sussex, Kent, London, Herts., Essex): Miss Sophie Rex, Denbigh Lodge, Shalford, Guildford, Surrey.

ORIENTEERING

9. The North East Orienteering Association (Durham and Northumberland): Miss T. Jack, 3 Helmsley Road, Newton Hall, Durham.
10. Yorkshire and Humberside Orienteering Association: Mr. Alan Ross, 29 Heworth Hall Drive, York. YO3 OAG

There are many Orienteering Clubs formed now, and the Regional Secretaries will be pleased to send you a list of Clubs in your area. The Annual membership fee, which will cover your Club, Regional and National affiliations, will be about 20s. for Seniors and Intermediates, or about 10s. for those in full-time education and the under-18's.

'. . . *farm stock should not be disturbed.*'

Bibliography

1. *The Sport of Orienteering*—by Stig Hedenström and Bjorn Kjellström. Written in English for the North American market. It has some good sections on compass and map practices. Published by Silva Ltd., Toronto, Ontario, Canada. 1955.

2. *Be Expert with Map and Compass*—by Bjorn Kjellström. Written in English for the American market. Well illustrated and dealing mostly with map and compass skills, rather than the competitive sport of orienteering. Available from B. J. Ward, Ltd., 130 Westminster Bridge Road, London, S.E.1. 1955.

3. *Orienteering*—produced by the Scottish Orienteering Association. A well-produced booklet which deals with map and compass work and the sport. Maps that are reproduced in the correct colours make the examples clear to follow. Published by 'Know the Game', Educational Publications. 1965.

4. *Nya Banläggar-boken*—the Swedish Official Handbook on orienteering. Various authors for each section of the book. Although written in Swedish, the many diagrams are self-explanatory.

5. *Skärmen*—the Year Book of Orienteering in Sweden. A well-produced record of all major competitions during the year, with coloured maps of the championship courses. Available from the Svenska Orienteringsförbundet, Tegnerg 36 C Uppsala, Sweden.

6. *Treningsboka*—by Willy Lorentzen. Written in Norwegian. A long chapter on training would be worth while having translated.

ORIENTEERING

7. *Orientierungs-wettkampfe*—Edited by Dr. Edelfrid Buggel. Written in German. A comprehensive book on the competitive sport. Published by Sportverlag Berlin, German Democratic Republic.

8. *Orientierrungslauf*—by various authors. A Swiss handbook, written in German and containing sections on all aspects of the sport. Published by Roman Bussman.

9. *The Silva Compass Instructional Pamphlet*—a concise leaflet on how to manipulate the compass, and obtain bearings from a map. To be found in every 'Silva' compass box.

10. *Hints on Orienteering*—by Christian Schaanning. Describes some of the more erudite techniques of way-finding in difficult country and orienteering procedures.

11. *Orienteering—A Unit Commander's Guide to the Sport*—by Captain Roger Chapman. Designed for Service use but containing much pertinent information for any orienteering situation.

'. . . *physical fitness is an integral part of orienteering*'.

Copying Services

1. Rank Xerox (Electro-static process).
   Cost per 100 copies: £3 15s. 0d.
   (At this price copies will be produced by return post or while you wait.)
      London office: Remax House, 31/32 Alfred Place, Store Street, London, W.C.1. Other Service Facilities in Birmingham, Manchester, Newcastle-on-Tyne, and Glasgow.
2. Office Printing Services,
   21 Stafford Street, Edinburgh.
   £5–£8 per 1,000 copies.
3. Printrite, 49 St. George's Walk, Croydon.
   Size 11 in. × 8 in. Cost 13s., plus 8s. per 100 copies.
   Very quick postal service.
4. Swift print of New Malden,
   84–86 Colliers Wood, High Street, London, S.W.19.
   Highly recommended by B.O.F. officials.
   £3 for 250 copies; paper size 10″×8″. One week's notice required.

PLEASE NOTE: As the reproduction of Ordnance Survey Maps is governed by the sanction of the Controller of H.M. Stationery Office, some proof will be necessary that permission has been sought before these firms will agree to do the work.

Duke of Edinburgh's Award Scheme

FITNESS SECTION: ORIENTEERING

This activity may be offered as part of the Fitness Section at Silver and Gold Stages of the Scheme. The candidates will be judged by the Assessors of the British Orienteering Federation, in accordance with the following conditions:

1. Practical Test. Candidates should in the period that they are engaged in the Award Scheme achieve the following standard in practical Orienteering. They must achieve this standard in at least *two* open races approved by the British Orienteering Federation.

Note. Most of the competitions that are indicated on the Regional and National Fixture Lists will be acceptable; however, Score Events will not be counted, neither will events be considered where boys enter and compete in pairs. This will probably bar night events for boys competing in Junior Races.

Silver Award. (*a*) For boys under 15—to achieve a time which is better than the average of the first three boys home plus 50 per cent of this time in a Boys/Girls class (under 15 on the day of competition) cross-country Orienteering competition. E.g.:

1st	Williams	40 min. 23 sec.
2nd	Clarke	46 min. 05 sec.
3rd	James	47 min. 38 sec.

Average $= \dfrac{134 \text{ min. } 06 \text{ sec.}}{3} = 44$ min. 42 sec.

ORIENTEERING

∴ Award Pass Time = 44 min. 42 sec. +
22 min. 21 sec. =
_____
67 min. 03 sec.

(*b*) For boys over 15—to achieve a time which is better than the average of the first three boys plus 75 per cent of this time in a Junior (over 15 and under 19 on the day of competition) cross-country Orienteering event.

Gold Award. Boys must achieve a time which is better than the average of the first three boys plus 50 per cent of this time in a Junior cross-country Orienteering competition.

2. Theory Test. Examiners appointed by the British Orienteering Federation will conduct an oral test for those candidates who have successfully completed the Practical Test. Where possible this test will be held in conjunction with an Orienteering event.

The questions asked in the test will relate to the following aspects of Orienteering:

(*a*) Types of Event—cross-country, score, line, night, etc., the general organization of these events, team scoring, relay work.

(*b*) The Rules of Competition.

(*c*) Control Terminology and definition of features.

(*d*) Techniques and skills—choice of routes, use of guide-lines, aiming-off, collecting-features, step-counting, height v. distance, rough v. smooth, etc.

(*e*) Training—map and compass techniques, physical fitness.

(*f*) Course setting—suitable country, control siting, selecting problems, positioning, the markers, etc.

(*g*) Country Code, Orienteering code of conduct and safety.

(*h*) Equipment.

(*i*) History and present state of the sport in this country.

Candidates will be expected to be reasonably knowledgeable about all the above aspects of the sport, and to be able to answer straightforward questions, not only about competing, but also about the organization of an event.

All communications on this aspect of the Duke of Edinburgh's Scheme should be addressed to the appropriate Regional Secretary. (*See* Appendix II.)

167

Index

Aiming-off, 73, 74
Amateur Athletic Association, 19, 24
Amateur status, 24
Assembly area, 141

Bannister, Dr. Roger, 21
Bearings, 52–61
  back, 63–4
B.O.F., 25, 122, 123
Brasher, Christopher, 21, 24

Calling-up station, 142
Charnley, Gerry, 20, 23
Choice of route, 68–71, 115–18
  unfair, 117
Clayton-le-Moors Harriers, 20
Clothing, 98–9, 130
Code of conduct, 49, 90
Collaboration, 131
Collecting features, 73
Compass, 51, 52, 99
  practices, 94
Constitution of the B.O.F., 156–9
Continuous running, 149
Contours, 47, 48
Control card, 33, 136
  markers, 36, 103, 104
  site, 119, 120, 144
  terminology, 82–4
Copier machines, 105–6
Copying services, 165
Copyright of maps, 50
Cross-country orienteering, 81, 123

Definition of controls, 82
Designation of controls, 121
Distance determining, 75
Dog-leg angles, 114
Double-step scale, 76

Duke of Edinburgh's Award Scheme, 166
Dyson, Geoffrey, 25

E.O.A., 23, 24, 25.
Equipment, 35, 85, 86, 98–108, 130

Fartlek, 150
Firbank, Thomas, 19
Finish, 144–5
Finland, 25
First commandment, 37, 92
Forestry Commission, 49
Four-right-angles technique, 65–6

Guide line features, 72
Grids, 42

Headlamp, 102
Height v. Distance, 71
Holmer, Gösta, 25, 150
Hunt the Silver Dollar, 95
Hyman, Martin, 21, 23

International Orienteering Federation, 18, 25
Interval running, 148

Killander, Major Ernst, 16
Kjellströms, 51
Kohvakka, Erkki, 18

Lagerfelt, Baron 'Rak', 18
Lindkvist, Ulla, 18
Line orienteering, 89–90
Lysfad, Magne, 18

Magnetic variation, 49, 54, 56
Marginal information, 41

169

INDEX

Marking stamps, 103
Master-maps, 34, 143

Night orienteering, 84–7, 132

Occasional orienteers, 23, 41
Ordnance survey maps, 33, 39, 40, 41, 46
  purchase of, 103–5
Organizing of an event, 135–6

Pendle Forest O.C., 20
Pirie, Gordon, 21
Point orienteering, 94
Private property, 91, 130
Prizes, 129
Protests, 133, 134

Recorder's sheet, 137
Relay racing, 87–9
Rendezvous site, 141
Rescue service, 129
Results board, 107
Romer, 44–6
Route cards, 138
Royalties, 106–8
Rules of competition, 123–34
Run-in, 118

Running training, 148–52

Safety, 86
Scale, 42
Score orienteering, 78–9, 139–40
Scotland, 18, 19
S.C.P.R., 19
Setting the map, 62–3
SILVA compass, 51–2, 99–101
Six-figure reference, 43–5
South Ribble O.C., 19–20, 23
Southern Navigators, 23
Start area, 141–3
Step-counting, 75
  scale, 76
Surrey, 21
Sweden, 17, 18

Tachometer, 102
Team competition, 80, 133
Terrain negotiating, 151
Thommen, Margrit, 18
Training diary, 152–3
  games, 93, 95–7
Tulloh, Bruce, 21, 23

Vetting, map and course, 125

Westbrook, Graham, 21